RETIRE
RICH
FROM REAL ESTATE

A Low-Risk Approach to Buying Rental Property
for the Long-Term Investor

MARC W. ANDERSEN, PhD

SPHINX® PUBLISHING
AN IMPRINT OF SOURCEBOOKS, INC.®
NAPERVILLE, ILLINOIS
www.SphinxLegal.com

First Edition: 2008

Published by: **Sphinx® Publishing, An Imprint of Sourcebooks, Inc.®**

<u>Naperville Office</u>
P.O. Box 4410
Naperville, Illinois 60567-4410
630-961-3900
Fax: 630-961-2168
www.sourcebooks.com
www.SphinxLegal.com

This publication is designed to provide accurate and authoritative information in regard to the subject matter covered. It is sold with the understanding that the publisher is not engaged in rendering legal, accounting, or other professional service. If legal advice or other expert assistance is required, the services of a competent professional person should be sought.
From a Declaration of Principles Jointly Adopted by a Committee of the American Bar Association and a Committee of Publishers and Associations
This product is not a substitute for legal advice.
Disclaimer required by Texas statutes.

Library of Congress Cataloging-in-Publication Data

Andersen, Marc W.
  Retire rich from real estate : a low-risk approach to buying rental property for the long-term investor / by Marc W. Andersen. -- 1st ed.
      p. cm.
  Includes bibliographical references.
  ISBN 978-1-57248-646-1 (pbk. : alk. paper) 1. Real estate investment. 2. Rental housing--Management. I. Title.

HD1382.5.A545 2007
332.63'24--dc22

Printed and bound in the United State of America.
SB — 10 9 8 7 6 5 4 3 2 1

Dedication

I dedicate this book to my wife, partner, and "chief" land-lady, Birgit, for her continuous support over the years. I thank her for listening to the endless conversations about real estate over the last fifteen years. She is the bright light of reason that steps in when I let emotion interfere with business. I also wish to express special thanks to my two older brothers, Ed and Eric, for providing an "umbrella" when I was younger and helping me find my way in life. It was their early success in real estate investing that motivated me and kept me from selling during the tough times.

CONTENTS

Introduction xiii

Chapter One: To Buy or Not to Buy 1
  The Benefits—Making Money Takes Time
  Cash Flow
  Appreciation
  Leverage
  Amortization
  Tax Advantages
  Time is Money
  Just the Facts—The POMS Survey
  The Costs—You Must Be Committed
  The POMS in Perspective—Why Buy At All?
  Summary

Chapter Two: Demographics 101 13
  Who Are Your Tenants and Where Do They Live?
  Future Demand for Rental Housing
  The Shortage of Affordable Housing
  Summary

Chapter Three: Looking for Properties 21
  Working with Realtors and the MLS
  Working with a Buyer's Agent

Newspaper Ads
Driving Around
Tax Records and Mailings
Using Seller's Agents
Real Estate Investment Clubs
Summary

Chapter Four: The Preferred Property Types 31

Single-Family Homes
Multifamily Dwellings
Townhomes, Condominiums, and Mobile Homes
Student Rentals
Rooming Houses
Building Styles
Single-Level, Two-Story, Side-by-Side, and Over-Under Flats
Utilities, Bathrooms, and Parking
Converting Single-Family to Multifamily
New Construction
Modular Housing
Summary

Chapter Five: Choosing a Location 53

The Fundamentals
Cash Flow versus Location
Choosing Location Using GRMs
GRM Summary
Suburban Sprawl
Main Street or Dead-End Streets?
Student Housing
Appreciation and Growth Trends
Investing in High-Priced Markets
Summary

Chapter Six: Determining Cash Flow 73

Myth versus Reality
Determining Operating Expenses
Calculating Cash Flow
Effect of Interest Rates on Cash Flow
GRMs to Predict Cash Flow
Cash Flow Calculators
Determine the Market Rents
Appreciation Makes Up for Negative Cash Flow
Summary

Chapter Seven: Valuing Property 89

Methods for Valuing Property
The Comparative Sales Approach
The Capitalization Rate Approach—"Cap Rates"
Stated Cap Rates
Understanding Cap Rates
Cap Rates and Short-Term Financing
Future Trends
Using GRMs to Predict Value
Replacement Cost Approach
Putting it All Together
The Final Check—Is the Property Likely to Appreciate?
Real Estate Bubbles
Summary

Chapter Eight: Financing Your Investment 113

Fixed-Rate, Adjustable-Rate, and Interest-Only Loans
Understanding Amortization
The Five Rules of Financing Your Properties
The Low Down on No-Down Deals
Cash-Out Refinancing

Financing for a Fixer-Upper
Money Back at Closing
Owners versus Non-Owner Occupied Financing
Commercial Financing
Summary

Chapter Nine: Making the Offer and Taking Over 129

Pre-Offer Inspections
Make-Ready Cost Estimates
Be Prepared to Walk
Offer to Purchase Forms
The Offer
Disclosure Forms
Earnest Money
Be Careful of Contract Exclusions
Closing the Deal
Final Due Diligence and Taking Over
Post-Offer Inspections
The Tenants
Identifying Opportunities and Avoiding Problem Properties
Summary

Chapter Ten: Advertising and Renting 145

"For Rent" Signs
Using a Realtor
Internet Advertising
Student Rentals
Advertise at Market Rent
Rent Concessions and Keeping Tenants
Summary

Chapter Eleven: Managing Your Investments............. 153

Should I Manage Myself?
Screening Tenants
Prior References
Problem Tenants
Pets
The Right Lease
Enforce It
The Three Rules of Lease Enforcement
Repairs and Maintenance
Handling Minor Repairs
Painting
Bigger Jobs
What is Really Necessary?
Appliances: Used or New?
Landscaping
Renting to Students
Students and Leases
Summary

Chapter Twelve: Insurance 175

Property and Casualty Insurance
Policy Deductibles
Personal Property
General Liability Insurance
Business Owners Package
Reducing the Risks of Lawsuits
Mold
Claims Histories and the CLUE Report
Summary

Chapter Thirteen: Taxes and Rental Property 187

Historical Overview
Passive and Non-Passive Income and Losses
The $25,000 Exclusion Rule
Depreciation
Repairs and Improvements
Other Expenses
Schedule E
Lose the Paper and Calculator
Summary

Chapter Fourteen: Selling Your Property..... 203

Preparing for the Sale
Selling as Owner-Occupied Dwellings
Selling as Investment Properties
Pricing, FSBOs, and Realtors
Depreciation Recapture
Determining your Taxable Gain
1031 Tax Exchanges
Summary

Chapter Fifteen: Bookkeeping and Computers 213

Organizing
One Bank Account
Financial Computer Programs
Summary

Glossary 219

Appendix A: Total Operating Expenses 235

Appendix B: Maintenance, Repairs, and
            Reserves.................... 237

Appendix C: Typical Computer-Generated
            Cash Flow (Report for Duplex) . . 243

Appendix D: Inspection Report 245

Appendix E: Maintenance Cost as a
            Percentage of Income......... 249

Notes 250

Index 253

INTRODUCTION

Real estate investing has been and will likely remain the single most effective means to achieve wealth. *Fortune Magazine* states that 97% of all self-made millionaires have made their fortunes from investing in real estate. Given the riches that have been made in real estate, you may be surprised to learn that, according to U.S. Census studies, only four out of ten private landlords that owned rental property were profitable in the year surveyed. As an investor who also struggled with cash flow in the early years, I was startled to learn this "unpublicized" statistic. Despite all the books, infomercials, and courses by real estate "gurus," the message is clear: *the average investor in real estate is not successful and continues to make the wrong investment decisions.*

In my early years of investing, I too was unprofitable and suffered with negative cash flow properties. It was my unwavering belief in real estate that kept me going and motivated me to identify the reasons behind this surprisingly high failure rate. As both a scientist and an investor, I was especially surprised at the lack of data available to make educated decisions about cash-flow predictions when purchasing property. The examples provided by the real estate investment gurus were typically the $100,000 houses that rent for $1,000 per month. As these high cash-flow properties are not largely found, I was troubled when confronted with "real life" situations; a four-unit apartment building is listed at $300,000 with gross rents of $2,400 per month. How do I estimate the yearly operating costs, such as maintenance and repairs? Will it have a positive cash flow at these rents and if so, what type of financing should I get? Although I read many of the books available, I still had no idea how to answer these questions. In a housing market where high property values and low rents were the norm, the "old" assumptions no longer applied. In short, there were no *tools* available to private investors to analyze such "real life" situations. It was these shortcomings and the persistent negative cash flows that motivated me to find the answers to these basic questions.

After years of research and hardships, I have identified the common pitfalls that affect the beginner investor and I have learned how to consistently beat the odds. In this book I present surprising research findings and simple tools for predicting profitability when buying investment property.

Creating wealth from real estate is a long-term proposition and the road is long and treacherous. It is not realistic to think you can make your fortune overnight. Once you make the right purchase you must learn how to hold on to and effectively manage your property. Because of this, a large portion of this book is dedicated to sharing our hard-earned lessons learned from our years in the business. By learning from the mistakes we made along the way, you will be able to avoid the common mistakes that lead to the high-observed failure rate of beginner investors. Use of the management techniques presented in this book should enable you to hold on to your properties for the long term as you watch your wealth grow year by year.

If you are worried about securing your financial future and you are thinking about buying your first rental property, then this book is for you. Application of these simple techniques will ensure that you make the *right* decisions and guarantee that your investing experience will build wealth and secure your retirement.

To Buy or Not to Buy

With few exceptions, the bulk of information on real estate investing presented in books, courses, and seminars addresses only the upside of investing in rental property. The palm tree backdrops and Bermuda shorts in the late-night infomercials create an illusion of easy money. After all, does anything sell better than the next get-rich-quick scheme? When we hear about these success stories we always ask ourselves the same question: "Could this work for me too?" The short answer is yes, you most certainly can get rich following their advice. Do people win the lottery every day? Yes, they do that as well. Unfortunately though, *neither* occurrence is typical, nor do they fall within the odds of normalcy. Donald Trump perhaps captured this best by saying, "Real estate is always good, *as far as I am concerned.*" The take-home message is that unless you are one of the fortunate few, the odds are against you being successful. Although we will learn that the odds of success *are* indeed stacked against you, the good news is that there is little investment risk to those investors who possess the necessary information to make the right decisions.

The Benefits—Making Money Takes Time

Investing in the stock market has certainly resulted in many lost fortunes, especially in recent years. You don't, however, typically hear of similar woes in real estate investing. That doesn't mean it doesn't happen, it just means the likelihood is lower, especially if you hold on for the long term. This is the key to gaining wealth in real estate investing. Like the stock market, where day traders have a higher risk of failure as compared to those who hold for the long term, so is the case with real estate investing. There are no doubt fortunes to be made by buying and selling real estate more quickly, or *flipping* properties. Such activities, however, are speculative and are therefore not really investments at all. If you are after the quick dollar, I recommend buying one of the many books on the subject. This book, however, is designed for the investor who plans to buy, hold, and build a portfolio of real estate over at least a ten-year period. We will go on to show that if you buy sensibly and hold on to your investments, your risks in fact are quite low. In the sections that follow, I summarize the five reasons why real estate has been a lucrative investment over the long haul.

> NOTE:
> A knowledgeable and well-informed real estate investor will nearly always beat the odds. The same cannot be said of investing in the stock market, where the majority fails to match the performance of a random dart throw.

Cash Flow

One of the greatest benefits of owning real estate is the potential income you can receive in the form of *cash flow*. *Cash flow* is simply the income left over after you pay all expenses on your rental properties. The expenses would include all charges associated with owning the property, including your monthly loan payments. Cash flow is therefore your *return on investment* (ROI) and is analogous to the percent yield you would obtain from a bank.

You obviously need your cash flow to be positive—or at worst break-even—otherwise your properties will drain money from you over time. A great benefit of cash flow is that it can increase over time from inflation. Rents over any ten-year period have largely increased, making it very likely that if you hold, your cash flow will only go up. But as we will see, cash flow is just one of many benefits awaiting the patient investor.

> **NOTE:**
> If you own ten units that rent for an average of $500 per unit, an annual increase in rents from inflation of just 3% over ten years results in an additional $1,000 of income per month, after adjusting for expenses. Interestingly, this $1,000 per month is just below the current average Social Security benefit.

Appreciation

There are two forms of property value appreciation. One form of appreciation is the increase in property values over time due to inflation. The second form of appreciation is where market value increases due to supply and demand factors. Indeed, it is a rare city or metropolitan area these days that has not seen increases far exceeding the rate of inflation. The national average for property appreciation of single-family homes in 2005 was 14%, or 10% above the rate of inflation. Although such high increases in property values are not consistent with expectations, historical home appreciation has still outpaced consumer price inflation.[1] As land becomes scarcer, the demand factor should continue to keep property values ahead of the rate of inflation.

Leverage

Leverage refers to the practice of buying something with a small down payment using a large amount of borrowed money or *debt*. *Debt* is a very bad thing when applied to *depreciating* assets. When applied to *appreciating* assets like real estate, debt has distinct benefits. With leveraged investments, small increases in property values translate to large returns on your initial down payment. As we will learn, however, the key factor in deciding how much to put down on your property will be determined by its cash flow potential. In general, the goal should be to minimize the amount you put down on a property (maximize your leverage) without going into a negative cash flow situation. Most banks or mortgage brokers require that the buyer purchase *mortgage insurance* if the *loan to value* (LTV) goes above 80% (less than 20% down) on residential investment properties. If the bank feels you are taking a risk and requires you to buy extra insurance, it seems reasonable to assume that you may be taking a risk. For these reasons and others, I advocate keeping a minimum of 10% down (90% LTV) on investment properties. This is a good balance between maximizing leveraging and minimizing risk. As we will learn in later chapters on cash-flow determinations, the biggest challenge we face as investors is learning how to maximize leveraging power without going into a negative cash flow situation.

Inflation + Leveraging = High Profits
While inflation lifts property values, it also raises your cost of living. In short, this means that if you have 100% equity in your property (zero leverage), your profits from inflation appreciation may be canceled by your inflating expenses. In reality, however, most investors leverage their cash. The following two cases illustrate the advantages of inflation appreciation when you leverage your cash.

Case 1: Unleveraged Investing
John puts a 100% down payment in real estate worth $100,000 and inflation is 3% per year. John thus earns $3,000 per year on his investment, or 3%. This 3%, though, is off-set by a 3% rise in John's cost of living expenses. Thus adjusted for inflation, John's return is zero.

(continued)

Case 2: Leveraged Investing
John's smarter sister Jane buys the house next door for the same price, but only puts $20,000 (20%) cash down instead of 100%. Inflation remains at 3% per year, so Jane also earns $3,000 per year. Since Jane only invested $20,000, however, Jane earns a 15% return on her investment ($3,000 / $20,000). This is known as the *power of leveraging*. For this reason, many investors prefer to keep their cash equity low in rental property so as to take full advantage of this added benefit of appreciation through inflation.

Amortization

When you borrow money in the process of leveraging, another advantage presents itself, namely *amortization*. Amortization is the process of paying both principal and interest on a loan that has a fixed period, for example fifteen or thirty years. Every month your total payment is fixed, but the principal part goes toward paying down your loan. This regular principal payment each month lowers your debt slowly and steadily over the fixed term so that you build equity and eventually you owe nothing on your property. This loan reduction over time is known as its *amortization schedule*. Over many years, amortization is a great benefit, especially when you consider that it is the tenants who are paying down your loan, not you.

Tax Advantages

Typically, in at least the first five years of owning rental property you will actually pay less tax than you would pay if you didn't own any rental property at all. This tax benefit of owning rental property is sort of the icing on the cake, so to speak. You shouldn't buy real estate just because of the tax advantages, but you should be aware that all these great benefits do not come with a tax penalty.

Time is Money

All these benefits of owning real estate—the increased cash flows, gains from appreciation, and mortgage pay-down—only come to those who are patient. Building wealth and letting money work for you is a slow and, at times, immeasurable process. In order to be successful you must be dedicated and committed for the long haul. A recent study from the *National Association of Realtors* (NAR) supports this. For instance, the typical homeowner who experiences an annual home appreciation rate of 5% and who made a cash-down payment of 10% will generally receive a 94% return on that cash after owning the home for three years. After owning a house for five years, a homeowner can expect a rate of return on the down payment to increase to 225%; after ten years, the rate of return jumps to 623%!

Understanding the benefits of owning real estate won't prepare you, however, for the arduous road ahead. One needs to know the potential pitfalls as well as the benefits. As George Washington said before the battle of Trenton: "One must know thy enemy in order to defeat him."

Just the Facts—The POMS Survey

The *Property Owners and Managers Survey* (POMS)[2] was the first known national survey of property owners and managers in the United States. This study collected information from over 16,000 owners and managers of privately held rental properties. Publicly held (i.e., governmentally owned) rental properties were not included in the survey. The data collected from this survey allowed researchers to analyze characteristics by the number of rental units or the number of properties. This report is the first of its kind to use the number of properties as the unit of analysis. The POMS report thus provides information on all property owners, from small investors (1–5 units) to large apartment owners (more than 50 units).

The POMS report provides the first real insight on landlords and provides actual data on their successes and failures. The study provides answers to questions on many topics that, to date, have been left to speculation. For example: Are rental property owners making money or losing money on their investments? Who is the typical owner of rental property? How much are owners paying on maintenance? In short, this study takes the guesswork out of finding answers to these critical questions. The following sections are based in part upon data taken from this study.

The Costs—You Must Be Committed

Regardless of whether you manage your properties yourself, you *will* be involved in your investment. Your properties will be a part of your life and *will* change your lifestyle. But don't take my word for it; rather, read what thousands of private investors have to say about owning rental properties. According to the POMS study, the feedback from the property owners is not so rosy and it certainly does not paint a picture of a palm tree and Bermuda shorts backdrop. From a random sampling of landlords nationwide, the following statistics were noted:

- About 32% of the owners of 1–49 units would *not* buy the [same] property again if given a second chance.

- About 50% of the owners of 1–49 units spent 1–8 hours every week on maintenance or management.

- About 20% spent *more* than 8 hours per week on maintenance or management.

- About 93% of respondents for all multifamily properties reported doing some type of work to specific rental units in the last five years.

- About 84% planned on renovating or replacing units in the near future.

The bottom line is that if you invest in rental property you must be committed. You *will* need to make decisions—*important* decisions—about your future and the future of your tenants. Even if you use a management company, don't think for a minute your manager will make these decisions without your input. Your management firm works for you. You are their boss. If they are good, they will at least provide you with several good options to choose from. But you are the one that will need to decide whether to collect partial payment of rents or proceed with eviction; whether to evict a tenant when you have discovered an illegal pet or negotiate an increased rent. As we can see from the survey, not everyone is willing to take on these responsibilities if given a second opportunity. Not everyone's personality is thus suited for this type of a job. Before you decide, though, let's look at some more data taken from the POMS study.

Why Do Investors Buy Rental Property?

For the owners of all categories of multifamily properties, whether single units or large apartment complexes, the primary reason for acquiring rental property was for the income from the rents. This ranged from a low of 32% for small properties to a high of 42% for medium-size and large properties. The responses for the second most common reason for acquiring rental property varied depending upon the size of the property. For small properties, use as a residence, meaning the owner either lives at the property or lived there when the owner bought the property, was equally as popular a reason for acquiring rental property as was income from rents. For medium-size and large properties, the second most common reason for acquiring rental property was for long-term capital gains. Surprisingly, only about 10% of those surveyed listed retirement benefits as a main reason to buy rental property.

Is Owning Rental Property Profitable?

Despite all the testimonials from late-night infomercials and get-rich-quick schemes, I was rather surprised to learn from the POMS study that many investors were not at all profitable in their investments. The following figure illustrates just how risky investing in rental property can be.

Profitability of Property Owners

Profits Last Year	Total	1–4 Units	5–49 Units	>50 Units
Yes, made a profit	41.4%	40.4%	45.9%	45.0%
No, broke even	16.2%	17.2%	12.7%	5.7%
No, had a loss	26.7%	27.9%	22.5%	3.0%
Don't know	15.7%	14.5%	18.9%	36.3%

Source: "Property Owners and Managers Survey" by U.S. Census 2000.

Overall, only 41% of multifamily property owners made a profit in the year of the survey. This left about 16% breaking even, 27% reporting a loss, and 16% who did not know whether they made or lost money. Interestingly, for single- family home investors, fully 46% either lost money or broke even and only 37% in this type of rental property actually made a profit.

The data is surprising, as it would seem to indicate that your odds of being profitable when you buy a rental property are not much better than fifty-fifty.[3] Apparently, buying that house or duplex next door and renting it for profit isn't as simple as it appears.

Why Do Owners Hold on to Rental Property?

One might think the reasons for holding on to rental property would be the same reasons for buying the property in the first place, which is only partially true. Regardless of the size of the property, all multi-family owners stated their primary reason for continuing to own property was the income they received from rents, the same reason they originally bought the property. The second most popular reason for owners of small properties was to use the property as a residence for themselves or their family. For owners of medium-size properties, the second reason was for retirement security, and for owners of large properties, it was for long-term capital gains. Note that retirement was a distant third reason why owners bought in the first place; yet when asked why they are keeping the property, that reason rose to second place. Thus, there is some glimmer of hope after all. Apparently the ones who are successful *now* feel owning the properties will provide some needed income in years to come.

Who is the Typical Property Owner?

Most properties, regardless of size, were owned by individual or partnership owners. Individual owners include single persons, husbands and wives, and trustees for estates of deceased persons. Partnerships include limited partnerships and general partnerships. Almost all small properties—96%—were owned by these two groups. For small properties, 92% were owned by individual owners, compared to 77% for medium-size properties, and 32% for large properties. About half of the multifamily properties owned by individuals or partnerships had owners between 45 and 64 years of age. Most rental property owners were white (85%). Black or African American individuals owned 8% of multifamily properties, Asian or Pacific Islanders owned 4%, and Hispanic individuals owned 6% of multifamily properties. This disparity in ownership between whites and minorities grew larger as the property size increased. Whites owned 93% of large multifamily properties, while Blacks and Hispanics owned only 1% and 2%, respectively.

The POMS in Perspective—
Why Buy at All?

So let me try and understand what this study is saying. In a National Survey of over 16,000 private landlords, the indisputable facts are that one in three owners would *not* buy the property again if given the chance and that less than one-half of the owners reported a profit on their investments. So why buy at all given these facts?

Because investing in real estate is the single best opportunity we have to build wealth.

One thing I think would change if the POMS study was updated is that we would find that the percentage of owners who are investing for their retirement would surely be elevated. Corporate pensions in the United States have largely vanished over the last ten years. Because of this, the baby boomer generation will need to rely on a combination of individual retirement plans, 401(k)s, and Social Security to provide for their retirement. If lucky, these savings will be adequate, but in many cases I fear they will not. Investing in real estate may be our only hope to achieve financial independence if we haven't (or can't) achieve wealth through a day job.

In the following chapters we will go on to provide a recipe for being a conservative yet highly successful investor. If you follow these simple yet practical guidelines, and keep at it for years to come, you will reach that point in your life where "Eureka"—you *suddenly* realize you have no more retirement worries!

Summary

- The benefits of owning real estate are cash flow, appreciation, loan reduction by your tenants, leveraging, and tax advantages.

- The POMS study was a national survey of over 16,000 property owners and provides for the first time accurate data about owners of multifamily properties.

- The POMS study indicated that less than half of the owners surveyed reported a profit on their properties.

- The POMS study indicated that half of the owners of small apartments (1–49 units) spent 1–8 hours every week on maintenance or management.

- In order to realize the benefits of owning real estate and to build wealth you must be committed and hold your properties for a long period of time.

- Despite the apparent risks and challenges, investing in real estate remains the single best opportunity we have to build wealth and secure our retirement.

DEMOGRAPHICS 101   2

The key to being a successful investor and landlord is understanding your tenant market. Paying attention to demographic trends is thus a must for any prospective wealth-builder. The word "demographics" stems from the Greek work *demos*, or "people." It is the statistical study of population with respect to age, sex, marital status, family size, education, geographic location, and occupation. Many demographic trends are quite easy to determine. If, for example, the birth rate increases during certain years (as indeed happened during the baby boom years), we can determine that there will be an increase in the demand for baby food and diapers. In several years there will be an increase in the demand for toys and children's clothes; after a decade an increased demand for public education, video games, and music CDs; after two decades an increased demand for university services, compact automobiles, rental apartments, wedding photographers, and furniture; after four decades an increase in the demand for houses, sedan cars, insurance, weight-loss centers, and investment services; after six decades an increased demand for health-care services and undertakers. In short, demographics and what they teach us are big business. Have you ever noticed that where you see one McDonald's restaurant on a corner, you usually find a Burger King, then a Wendy's right across the street? There is actually a reason for this. The first franchise to arrive picked that location based upon a demographic marketing study they conducted of that area. These studies are expensive and can cost up to several hundred thousand dollars. After the first franchise arrives, it does not take long for other franchises to arrive and take advantage of these prime locations without having to pay for the expensive marketing studies.

We are fortunate in our great land that we can actually access quite a lot of data for no cost at all. The figures that we are going to look at are from the U.S. Census Bureau and are thus already paid for by your tax dollars. They are, in fact, very informative and provide valuable insight into current and future market trends in the U.S. rental housing market. Knowing their tenants' gender, income levels, where they work, how many children they have, and their ages helps landlords plan for demand and thus profitability. In short, if you know and understand your customers, you can provide them with the services they seek.

Who Are Your Tenants and Where Do They Live?

The last U.S. Census (2000) showed that about 66%, or two out of three people, owned their own home in the United States. The proportions varied depending on whether these people were from suburban areas or larger cities. In large inner cities, renters actually outnumbered owners (e.g., 70% in New York City and 61% in Los Angeles); however, in rural and suburban areas owners reached as high as 75%[4]. With 34% of our population living as tenants, the next question is, who are they and where do they live? As can be seen from the following figure, as of 1999, of the total of 34% of renters, 36% lived in single-family homes, 21% rented smaller (2–4 unit) buildings, and the remaining 43% lived in multiunit (> 5 unit) apartment complexes.

Who Lives Where

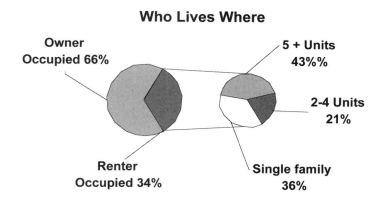

Owner Occupied 66%

5 + Units 43%%

2-4 Units 21%

Renter Occupied 34%

Single family 36%

a Adapted from Jack Goodman, "The Changing Demography of Multifamily Rental Housing," u*Housing Policy Debate* 10.1, 1999

The study also established that at least 70% of all of these renters rented out of necessity. In other words, they rent because they cannot afford the cost of an entry-level home. This leaves 30% who rent by choice. These renters, the ones who rent by choice, are the middle and upper-end income renters. This group of renters has been growing rapidly in recent years. As a result of this trend, apartment construction has increasingly targeted this group by building more upper-end, luxury-style apartments.

> **NOTE:**
> The 70% of the tenant population that rent out of necessity are the potential rental market for the small investor. The other 30% that prefer luxury apartments tend to live in the larger "community style" apartment complexes.

A recent study from Harvard University[5] further defined and categorized the rental market. Key to the study was the recognition of three categories, or markets, for renters in the United States: the affordable housing market, the middle market, and the so-called luxury renters, or lifestyle renter market.

Distributions of the Three Rental Markets

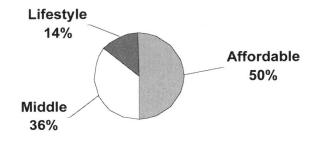

The first of these categories, affordable housing, serves the low-and moderate-income bracket. Essentially, these are the renters that *must* rent out of necessity. They pay more than 30% of their incomes toward the rent and at the time of the study earned a median income of $10,444 per year. The affordable market makes up 50% of the total market. This group tends to be older, non-white, less mobile, and tends to have at least one child. Almost half of the affordable housing group, or 39%, lives in some type of assisted housing (federal, state, or local).

The highest income bracket renters are the so-called lifestyle renters. Lifestyle renters comprise 14% of the market. In contrast to the affordable group, the lifestyle renters had a median income of $48,928 per year and 80% were non-minority. Lifestyle renters are typified by the fact that they have enough money to buy a house but *choose* to rent. This segment of the market was the fastest growing segment in the last U.S. Census.

Although the low- and high-income renters get much of the attention, the middle market comprises a full 36% of all renters. These renters tend to be younger and more mobile than the lifestyle and affordable renters. The typical middle market renter is a college graduate who has begun working but has not yet saved enough to buy a home. Also significant in this middle market category are single women with no children, single-parent households, and couples without children.

Future Demand for Rental Housing

Over a thirty-year period, from 1960 to 1990, home ownership had increased only 2%. In the ten years from 1990 to 2000, this rate tripled. This steep increase is due in part to the fact that current mortgage rates are the lowest they have been since the 1960s.

So with these trends toward home ownership, should we be investing in real estate at all? Current studies suggest the answer is yes. Although much attention has been paid to home ownership rates, at the same time, the number of apartment households is also growing. Recent studies by the Fannie Mae Foundation and Harvard University made the following conclusions. Both these studies predict that homeownership will probably not continue on its current rate of increase. The low interest rates and high consumer confidence that have boosted home purchases is already slowing. In addition to this, the homeowners' capital gains tax exclusion is predicted to foster apartment growth in the future. Unlike the earlier tax laws allowing only a single $125,000 gain, the new law allows large tax-free gains ($500,000) to be repeated every two years. This tax change opens up renting to a growing aging population who, under the old tax laws, had to remain in their home in order to avoid large capital gains from appreciation. All these findings point to the fact that *both* home ownership and apartment household growth is projected to go up at approximately the same rate in the next ten years.[6]

The fact that apartment growth will keep pace with homeowner growth seems at odds with all the baby boomers moving into middle age. Two important demographics, however, offset this baby boomer trend. First, the number of 20 to 29-year-olds—a key group for apartment residency—has begun increasing again. Second, the U.S. Census Bureau projects that adult residents of all ages will increasingly live by themselves and this trend will boost the need for apartments. The study[7] cites the following reasons for this predicted rate of apartment renting growth in the next ten years:

- Young adult renters will be increasing due to the *echo boomer generation* (born post-1977). These adults are delaying marriage and buying homes due to the higher mobility of today's workers.

- Census studies predict that the typical American family household will continue its decrease, being replaced with an increasing number of single adults and single-parent and childless couples. In fact, in the 1990s, single head of households accounted for fully two-thirds of all new households in the United States.

- Immigration is predicted to account for 25% of all household growth through 2010. Since more immigrants rent proportionally, this is predicted to account for 44% of the increase in renters from 1995 to 2010.

- Baby boomers will continue to give up their homes for simpler apartment living,

NOTE:
Lay-offs, down-sizing, and right-sizing are increasingly a "way of life" for today's worker. In response to this uncertain environment, a trend moving *away* from homeownership and toward the more flexible lifestyle of renting is not surprising.

The Shortage of Affordable Housing

Based upon these projections, there is also predicted to be an increasing need for affordable housing. Since most of the industry has been focused on the lifestyle renters and building to meet these demands, affordable housing needs have fallen short of demand. The federal government has countered this with the implementation of Section 8 programs and tax-credit incentives to investors who commit their properties to long-term affordable housing. These efforts, however, cannot make up for the last two decades in which federal assistance essentially leveled off or declined. The need for affordable housing will be expected to continue to exceed demand as the gap between the "haves" and the "have-nots" widens.

Summary

- At least 70% of all renters rent out of necessity because they cannot afford the cost of an entry-level home.

- The fastest growing household types between now and 2010 are predicted to be smaller households—single-adult households, childless couples, and single-parent households—all of which have a higher propensity to choose apartment living.

- The number of individuals seeking smaller housing units will be further increased as the echo boomers move out of their parents' homes and the baby boomers become empty nesters.

- The trend after 2010 will likely shift more toward older age groups, where population growth is expected to accelerate between now and 2025.

- Immigration is predicted to account for 25% of all household growth through 2010.

- As investors it is essential we understand national trends and how they manifest themselves at a local level.

- By knowing our customers through demographics we can better serve them and thus will be more successful in our investments.

LOOKING FOR PROPERTIES

3

The first part of our journey will begin with learning how to acquire the tools to effectively locate potential rental properties.

Working with Realtors and the MLS

By far, most investors still locate and buy rental property using the service of a real estate agent. When working with a *Realtor*—or buyer's agent—you would typically sign a six-month contract and the agent would then locate properties for you. With the advent of the Internet, however, signing on with a buyer's agent is far less critical than it was years ago. To understand why this is so, you must first understand the process by which residential property is listed and sold. When a person wishes to sell a property, he can either sell as "for sale by owner" (FSBO), or he can list the property with a real estate agent. When the property is listed with a Realtor, it gets posted on the *Multiple Listings Service* (MLS) by the listing (seller) agent. Although sellers are becoming increasingly more successful with FSBO approaches, most residential real estate is still sold through the MLS. The reason the MLS still dominates the sales market is that there is no other single database that accesses more potential buyers. The smart seller therefore will nearly always hire a real estate agent as his or her seller's agent or listing agent to ensure maximum MLS exposure to buyers. Typical seller's agent commissions on MLS properties in the United States range from 4% to 6% of the purchase price. If the seller's agent sells the property without the aid of a buyer's agent, the seller's agent typically gets to keep the full commission. If the seller's agent sells to a buyer who is represented by a buyer's agent, the seller will need to share his commission with the buyer's agent. The typical split is about one-half of the seller's commission. Obviously, it is in the seller's agents' interest to sell a property without the involvement of a second realtor. If they can accomplish this, they stand to gain thousands more in commissions. In years past, listing agents had many days to try and network and locate a buyer before the listing became public on the MLS, and thus was shared with other buyer's agents. Currently, however, the listing agent has only a one- to two-day period before he or she must, by law, post his or her property to the MLS. Once listed, the property is accessible by buyer's agents who represent buyers who are looking for investment property. The real estate commission cites that only about 5% of all sales are actually closed by the listing agent, meaning that seller's agents are not very successful in selling their properties in this short time frame before the listings are accessible to all other real estate agents.

Historically, it was always the case that if you wanted access to the MLS as a private buyer, you had to go through a real estate broker. With the advent of the Internet, this has changed. Approximately twenty-four hours after a seller's agent posts a property to the MLS, the data becomes available to the entire public on Realtor.com (**www.realtor.com**). The result is that private investors working without realtors can now access properties nearly as well as any realtor, save that initial 24- to 48-hour period before the seller's agent is obligated to post his or her listing on the MLS.

Since MLS properties can now be found on the Internet, the need to sign on with a buyer's agent is not as acute as it once was. After locating a property on **www.realtor.com,** you can simply call the listing agent directly and circumvent the need for a buyer's agent.

There are some advantages to this approach. If the listing (seller) agent sells the property without the involvement of another agent, he or she gets a higher commission. Therefore, all other things being equal, the seller's agent will have a vested interest in selling *you* the property when you declare that you are *not* working with a buyer's agent. This situation obviously can give you a competitive edge over buyers who are using buyer's agents. For a $200,000 property, the seller's agent would pocket $10,000 (5% commission) if he or she sells directly to you, or $5,000 (2.5% to the buyer's agent) if shared with a buyer's agent. This is a powerful advantage when another buyer shows up on the scene with a buyer's agent and you don't have one. You may find the seller's agent working hard on your behalf to convince the seller to sell to you, knowing he or she will pocket the full commission. Officially, of course, this preferential treatment isn't allowed. Unofficially, however, the higher commission may help drive a deal in your favor.

If you do decide to proceed without a realtor, be aware that some seller's agent contracts do not allow this *dual agency* where the listing (seller) agent can also act as a buyer's agent. Thus, if you contact a realtor and get the cold shoulder, it's a good bet the seller cannot show you the property unless you are represented by a buyer's agent. If this is the case they will usually tell you upfront that you need to be working with a realtor in order to see their listing. In addition to these dual agency exclusion situations, there are other circumstances where using a buyer's agent as a realtor can be valuable.

Working with a Buyer's Agent

Obviously, if you choose not to work with a buyer's agent, you need to be comfortable negotiating on your own, making offers, and filling out offers to purchase contracts. This can be quite daunting to a novice investor. If you do not feel comfortable navigating this alone, then it may make sense for you to work with a buyer's agent, at least until you become familiar with the buying process. A situation where you will absolutely need the assistance of a buyer's agent is when you are trying to locate a property in an extremely hot real estate market. In these cases, the 48 hours it takes for the listing to become posted on the Internet is too long and you will continually miss out on deals unless you have a realtor constantly monitoring the MLS listings for you. In such markets, a buyer's agent can give you a 24- to 48-hour jump on properties that hit the MLS.

If you do sign on with a buyer's agent, be sure to exclude FSBO properties in your agreement. If you have signed on with a buyer's agent and FSBOs were not excluded from your contract, the owner of the FSBO may not want to pay any realtor fees and thus you may be liable for these fees. Be sure to consult your contract carefully before contacting an FSBO seller if you are working with a buyer's agent. Also, if possible, try and work with buyer's agents who are especially trained in the area of investment real estate. They will display the *Certified Commercial Investment Member* (CCIM) title. Finally, you should be aware that there are buyer's agents out there known as *exclusive buyer's agents* or *buyer only* agents. These agents do not list properties themselves and therefore represent only the buyer's interests in a real estate transaction. Certainly working under such an agreement goes a long way toward having a buyer's agent give you proper representation. Be aware, though, that the seller is still paying his or her salary. Unless you have an arrangement where the buyer only agent collects a flat fee from you, the buyer, I would use caution and not share any information you feel may be of value to the seller.

In summary, the exact process of posting to the MLS as well as seller and buyer's agent commission schedules may be different in your area of the country. I therefore recommend you first familiarize yourself with the entire (MLS) sale process in the area you wish to invest. After this, you can then judge whether it makes sense to work with a buyer's agent or not. No matter what type of realtor you end up working with, my recommendation is that you do not disclose any information that you wouldn't want the seller to know.

Newspaper Ads

The local newspaper is still a good traditional source for locating properties. Be cautious, however, as properties listed by owner are often priced much higher than actual market values. The typical strategy is to *float* your property out there at a higher price to see if it can be sold without having to enlist a realtor and pay fees. In theory, the FSBOs should be selling at a 4%–6% discount, as the seller doesn't need to pay any commission. In reality however, human nature (greed) prevails, and advertised FSBOs are typically listed at higher than market value or more than what a realtor would list the property for. Remember, a realtor does not want to sit on a property for months with no commission. Because of this, he or she will think very carefully about market value and then price the property at a competitive level to ensure it sells fast.

When you call the number in a newspaper advertisement, ask specifically whether the seller is a real estate agent or not. If he or she is, he or she must disclose this by law. Tell him or her right up front that you are not working with a realtor. This should peak his or her interest, as he or she would get full commission from a sale to you. Another approach that is reportedly useful is posting a *real estate wanted advertisement* in the local newspaper. Although this technique is described in just about every book on real estate investing, I have had little success using this method, despite spending several hundred dollars running ads. This advertising method seems to attract sellers of problem properties.

Driving Around

By far, the best way to find rental property is to simply scout the target neighborhoods by driving around. In addition to finding properties for sale by realtors, you will also find FSBOs. Look for *For Rent* signs by owners. The owners of these properties can be contacted about the possibility of selling. If they don't want to sell, take the opportunity to find out what the rents are and what the neighborhood is like.

The important thing about using this technique is to be consistent and to drive through your target areas of investment at least once a week. If the market is hot, you may consider driving through more often. Not only is this technique an effective way to find properties, it also fulfills a very essential task. By driving through these neighborhoods you are likely acquiring important information on rents, vacancy factors, crime, and neighborhood demographics. This data will be critical later on when we need to calculate cash flows and assess risk factors. In short, by making regular visits, you are getting to know your target area of investment.

Tax Records and Mailings

Whether you obtain your property leads from the newspaper, the Internet, driving around, or using a realtor, you need to develop a good system for researching your leads. Your city or county tax records provide the information you will need, such as tax values, number of units, purchase date, square footage, and owner addresses. It used to be that realtors were the only source for this information, but the Internet has changed this. By now, nearly every county or city has online access to these records. Many websites even have pictures and comparative sales data. It is important that you become familiar with how to perform these searches.

In addition to providing valuable information on your lead properties, these online records provide a ready database of potential sellers. Many sellers are motivated by a quick sale where they don't need to pay realtor's fees or be exposed to inexperienced buyers. If the owner's address is listed as the same as the rental address, they may or may not live at the subject property. Many owners wish to remain anonymous and try to avoid listing their home address with the rental property. You may need to cross-reference the search by name to actually track down the owner's home address. Once you gather the addresses and names, send out a form letter to all the owners. Be sure to include in your letter that you are prepared to pay market value for their property and can close in thirty days. I used this approach on several occasions with great success. In one case, the target neighborhood I was interested in had no prior sales posted in over five years. Using this approach, I was able to buy a property in the area. When I sent my first round of letters I ended up with three leads. The first two were not serious sellers and were just testing the waters. The third call, though, was a motivated seller. Although I did pay full market price for the property, I would otherwise have had no opportunity to buy in the neighborhood.

This technique is really all about timing. After I bought this property, a second mailing precipitated more calls from interested sellers. Two properties had extensive deferred maintenance and we ended up buying one of them for below market value. When we were done with the renovation work, we had fully renovated units for around market value.

All these sellers had one thing in common. They preferred not to work with realtors and were looking for a quick closing with an experienced buyer. Many sellers simply cannot justify parting with thousands of dollars in commissions when selling through a real estate agency.

CAUTION:
When using this method of mass solicitation, you will invariably attract a high number of sellers with problem properties. These may or may not be good buying opportunities. When using this approach you need to ensure that you fully research each prospective property for any potential problems the seller may be hiding.

Using Seller's Agents

A great way to locate properties is by contacting seller's agents in your area who specialize in investment property. Recall from the previous section that the seller's agents have a window of 24 to 48 hours to sell their properties on their own before sharing the information with the public. Because of this window of opportunity most seller's agents will (gladly) take your name and contact you when they have a property to sell, so long as you are not working with a buyer's agent. Remember, if they sell to you directly, they get the full commission. Don't sign on with a seller's agent, however. If you sign on with a seller's agent then you are limiting property leads to just one agent. My preference is that I try not to sign any agreements with a seller's agent, and put my contact information with as many seller's agents as I can. This way I maximize my source of property leads. Typically property leads come in at a good rate after making these contacts.

If you do end up working with a seller's agent, remember that he or she is legally required to share with the seller any and all information you provide him or her. For this reason, do not ever divulge to a realtor how much you are willing to pay. Do your homework, present your offer, and keep things to yourself. Even if it isn't your bottom dollar offer, make that realtor believe it is.

Real Estate Investment Clubs

If you are a people person and enjoy mixing business with pleasure, a local real estate investing club may be a good way for you to find properties. Even if they don't provide any leads on properties, these clubs can be a great place to network and meet people who share a common interest with you. The best place to begin your search for such a club is through the *National Real Estate Investors Association* (National REIA). This is a nonprofit association made up of a federation of local associations or investment clubs throughout the United States. Currently they are the largest organization dedicated to the individual investor. With the recent explosive growth of local associations, there was a need for more professionalism, standards, and an organization for the sharing of ideas and information. The National REIA took on this role as a representative of the industry as a whole, becoming a resource to associations and their members.

Finding a local club can have many advantages. Unlike stock market investing clubs, where you pool your money and make joint invest-ments, real estate clubs are more about networking and education. The best clubs feature professional speakers such as local attorneys, mort-gage brokers, insurance agents, contractors, home inspectors, and other professionals in the business. This is a symbiotic relationship where local businesses get to pitch their products and novice investors can learn about real estate investment products and services offered in their area. Beware though; due to the recent popularity and growth in real estate investing, many of the newer clubs are *for profit* and often turn toward speakers that have something to sell. Such speakers rarely provide any educational content in return. Because of this discrepancy, look for a club that has been established for several years. If nothing else, I find these clubs an excellent place to vent and share war stories with fellow landlords. They can also be great places to learn from the seasoned landlords.

Summary

- Most investors still locate and buy rental property using the service of a real estate agent.

- You should not disclose any information to a real estate agent that you wouldn't want the seller to know.

- Accessing the multiple listing service (MLS) online through free providers such as **www.realtor.com** can provide a good resource for finding investment properties.

- Driving around a prospective neighborhood is an effective way to find properties and gain critical information on rents, vacancy factors, crime, and neighborhood demographics.

- Mass mailing private owners using available online tax records is an effective method to locate motivated sellers.

THE PREFERRED PROPERTY TYPES

4

There are many different types and styles of residential rental property available to the investor. There are single-family investments such as single-family homes, townhomes, and condominiums. There are multifamily structures such as duplexes, triplexes, quadraplexes, small apartment buildings, garden apartments, and high-rise apartments. Within these structure types there are diverse classes of tenants such as student housing, affordable and low- to mid-income housing, luxury housing, and rooming houses. There are also building styles to choose from such as over-under flats, side-by-side apartments, one story, two stories, high-rise, and structures built on a slab or a raised foundation. In short, there are many options to choose from.

This chapter provides valuable guidelines on how to select the right property types and building styles to invest in. Although the discussion will cover both single-family as well as multifamily properties, the emphasis will be on small apartment buildings of two to four units. As we will see again and again, these are the investments that bring the most value with the least risk. In particular, rental properties with up to four units can be purchased with conventional Fannie Mae and Freddie Mac loans and thus can be financed using long-term fixed-rate mortgages.

Structures having more than four units are considered commercial properties and cannot be purchased with conventional financing.

Due to the higher risk associated with these shorter-term commercial loans, these investments are reserved for more experienced investors. That is not to say that such commercial residential investments are inferior. In fact, I will show in later chapters that larger apartment buildings are typically the most profitable. I recommend, though, that the novice investor first gain experience with buying and managing non-commercial, smaller apartment buildings.

Single-Family Homes

There is no shortage of books, real estate courses, and infomercials promoting the investment in single-family homes as a wealth-building enterprise. This is largely due to the fact that buying a single-family home is a familiar process to most of us. History also shows that purchasing single-family homes and holding for the long term is basically risk-free, as evidenced by the steady increase in property values over the last forty years. Although the single-family home you live in may be a good long-term investment, investing in a single-family home as a rental property has many drawbacks. In fact, investing in single-family homes as rental property actually provides a far poorer rate of return than investing in multifamily properties. Due to their endearing popularity, however, I will list some of the benefits of investing in single-family homes:

- With single-family homes the tenant can often be made responsible for yard maintenance, providing more profit to the investor.

- Property appreciation is usually higher for single-family homes than with multifamily homes.

- The legal structure for buying, selling, and transferring title of single-family homes is well established and easy to understand.

- Financing for single-family homes is readily available and often at very favorable terms for the investor. One may not be required to pay investor interest rates, which are typically higher than owner-occupied rates.

The disadvantages of investing in single-family homes, however, are many. Cash flows for single-family homes are typically less than for multifamily units. The reason for this is that single-family homes cost more per unit than multifamily buildings because a greater proportion of the value is attributed to land. Since land provides no income you will always have a better cash flow with investments where the proportion of value from your building is high and land is low.

A huge disadvantage of owning single-family homes as rental property is when your house is vacant, you have a 100% vacancy rate. Having to pay a full mortgage payment every month during vacancy periods can quickly eat away your profits. At least with a duplex, triplex, or quadraplex, chances are lower that multiple units will be vacant at the same time.

It is true that single-family homes may appreciate more than multifamily homes. It is also true that to realize your profits from single-family home ownership you must eventually sell your property. But selling single-family homes is more difficult than selling a multifamily property. Buyers' expectations for single-family homes, either as owner-occupied or as investment properties, are typically higher than for multifamily, income-producing properties. In order to obtain market value for your single-family home, and thus to realize your appreciation gains, you must be prepared to spend a lot of money renovating, painting, and landscaping before marketing your home. This is especially true if the house has been used for many years as a rental property and you want to market it as an owner-occupied house. Often these necessary repairs will bite into your profits and offset any additional appreciation gains you might have had with these property types.

There is another more fundamental reason why single-family homes make poor investments. Since single-family homes are more expensive per unit than multi-unit housing, rents need to be proportionally higher to support the higher per unit cost. Demanding higher rents in today's rental market can be problematic. With the current climate of affordable interest rates, today's renters are increasingly able to afford their own homes. Even in higher interest rate environments, history has shown that lenders quickly adapt with more creative loan programs, making home ownership more affordable to lower income groups.

What implication does this have for the single-family home investor? If you are renting out a house, your potential pool of tenants can often afford to buy a house in that same neighborhood. These tenants are renting single-family homes for one of three reasons. First, they are new to the area and want to become familiar with their surroundings before buying. Second, they are renting because they can't obtain a loan due to credit issues. The third reason, and least likely, is that they just prefer to rent a house instead of owning one. At the risk of generalizing then, tenants of single-family rentals tend to be either *short-term* tenants (good credit but new to the area) or they tend to be *high-risk* tenants due to poor credit histories.

There are cases where single-family investments make sense. By far the best opportunity in the single-family home market is investing in houses you can buy cheap *and* rent cheap. For example, older, small, one- to two-bedroom homes located in the correct demographic area can often be bought at a price that attracts tenants who fall within the right income bracket (more on this later). In my area, for example, where starter homes begin at $120,000, a house you could buy for $60,000 and rent for $600 per month would make a great investment. Unfortunately, such deals are becoming increasingly harder to find as property prices continue to rise.

Another example of where a single-family rental may make sense is when you convert a home that you lived in to a rental property. Due to increased home equity and low interest rates, many homeowners can afford to keep their original home when they buy a new home. You may have a very low mortgage payment and thus can afford to accept lower rents necessary to attract and retain long-term tenants and still obtain a positive cash flow. If you do end up renting out the home you lived in, be sure you sell within three years so you can realize the current tax benefit and are exempt from paying taxes on capital gains. This follows from the recent tax law that states if you have lived in your home for two of the past five years you can take up to $500,000 ($250,000 for single households) in capital gains without paying taxes. You will have to pay back the depreciation you took on the house while it was rented, but you are still way ahead of the game. Be sure to consult an accountant, or one of the many tax programs available, to calculate these scenarios before making a commitment. When you weigh all the risks against the small chance of appreciation during this three-year window where you need to sell, you may decide it is not worth the risk.

Multifamily Dwellings

Given the current demographic trend of our country, and the movement toward 100% home ownership, one might ask whether rental property may become obsolete some day, and landlords an extinct race of beings, our long-tailed coats, pocket watches, key chains, and top hats fading into history. Whether or not this will happen, one thing is for certain: with the current environment of low-interest rates, interest-only loans, and hundreds of loan programs available for affordable housing, the pool of available renters is both decreasing *and* shifting toward a lower-income group. This trend has specific implications for investors of residential property. If the goal of the typical tenant is to own a home, then the rents you charge as a landlord should be well below the entry-level mortgage payments in your area. If your rents are close to this level, then you are marketing your property to future homeowners and not long-term renters. Consider this example: If one can buy a small starter home in your target area for $140,000, the mortgage payment will be approximately $800 (assuming a 6% interest rate, 30-year loan, 10% taxes and insurance). In this case, your pool of potential renters will get smaller as your rents approach this $800 level and exceed it. Ideally, the largest pool of renters will fall well below this number, perhaps in the $400–$700 per month range. It is for these reasons that multifamily dwellings make far better investments than single-family structures. The cost per unit discount gives rise to more affordable rents and thus a steady market for long-term renters. Additionally, as mentioned earlier, multiple unit buildings also carry less vacancy risk, as it is less likely that all units will be vacant at the same time. There is also the added value of having one insurance policy, one lot of land, one building to pay taxes on, and one roof to repair. All these factors contribute to a lower per unit cost and a better opportunity for positive cash flow even with lower rents. By targeting a pool of renters that is least likely to buy you will also have fewer tenant turnovers, which results in less make-ready costs between vacancies. The downside of renting to this group of tenants is that you need to be extra vigilant in your screening and qualifying of tenants.

To summarize, in order to target long-term renters, your rents need to be well below the cost of an entry-level mortgage payment for housing in your target area of investment. Single-family homes cost more per unit and can therefore not normally provide a positive cash flow at these lower rents. Typically, only multifamily properties will afford a positive cash flow at these rent levels.

Townhomes, Condominiums, and Mobile Homes

If you are paying attention to cash flow, chances are you will be eventually attracted to townhomes, condominiums, or mobile homes. All things being equal, cash flows are typically higher for these types of properties. In the case of townhomes and condominiums, the reason for this is that their market value is discounted because little (or no) land is included. As you do not own any land, an argument could be made that you own only depreciating assets, namely, brick, mortar, wood, etc. In reality then, any appreciation realized with these assets is largely due to speculation on location, and not due to land, which is a tangible asset. Another disadvantage of owning these types of investments is the homeowners' or condo association fees associated with this type of housing. Such fees can cut deeply into your profits and can increase without notice depending on the level of deferred maintenance in the building. I have heard of cases where a new parking area is required and fees suddenly increase. This increase in fees can make these properties hard to sell and less liquid. Another potential drawback in owning these investments is that your property's worth is only as high as the worst unit in the building. If the homeowners' association ceases to invest in the building or your neighbor begins to rent to less desirable tenants, the worth of your dwelling may depreciate in value as well. In large cities, however, where land is limited, these properties may be the only investment option available.

NOTE:
Although the building *depreciates* over time according to its useful life expectancy, in practice the inflation of building materials tends to offset losses from depreciation. I once looked at a quadraplex in an older, more established neighborhood. The owner told me he built it 30 years ago for only

$16,000. That same structure would cost over $300,000 in today's dollars to replace new. Even when one allows for depreciation due to its age, clearly an existing building can "appreciate" in value.

In the case of mobile homes, things are different, as you may own the land. Whereas the mobile home itself has a short usable life, if the home is used to pay off the land, it can be a good investment. You can't argue paying $20,000 for a used three-bedroom mobile home that you can put on a lot and rent for ten years at $600–$700 per month. Cash flows can be phenomenal. Be careful though, as mobile homes depreciate quickly. This is evidenced by the fact that they are priced based upon the year they were built, much like automobiles. Mobile homes also make sense when you find land you want to invest in but are not yet secure enough with the area to build on it. If local zoning laws allow, the addition of a mobile home can instantly provide income for an otherwise poor investment.

In summary, the recurring theme we will repeatedly revisit is that cash flow and risk are usually inversely proportional, meaning if one is high, the other is low. Condos and townhomes are no different. Additional homeowner fees and/or appreciation risks due to the lack of land associated with these investments invariably offset the higher cash flows.

Student Rentals

Whether you decide upon investing in single-family or multifamily units, if you live near a college or university, you may be interested in renting to students. Renting to students is such a different market that for the purposes of this book, student rental property is always discussed separately. Renting to students can provide many advantages over renting to non-students, some of which are listed below.

- Students provide a steady and increasing pool of tenants, less susceptible to economic downturns.

- Rents are always paid on time and usually backed by parents if necessary.

- Rents are higher when units can be rented by the room. For example, a single-family home rented by the bedroom will command a higher rent than what a family might pay.

- Students are more likely to respond to authority figures (the "landlord"), and therefore are usually more responsive to corrective actions.

The disadvantages to renting to students are:

- Tenant turnover is high. Although rents are higher, move-in/move-out fees and make-ready repairs are costly. These higher expenses can often erase any potential profits obtained from the higher rents.

- Units tend to undergo a high level of wear and tear, which the owner cannot charge for.

- Roommate conflicts can lead to unplanned vacancies if leases are not enforced.

- Students are less accustomed to apartment living, resulting in a higher number of service calls when compared to "seasoned" apartment renters.

- Student properties, especially in single-family (owner-occupied) neighborhoods, are a magnet for parties or other student congregations leading to complaints from neighbors.

- Due to the seasonal nature of renting to students, lease timing can be critical. If one misses the spring/summer leasing window, long-term vacancy may result until the following rental season.

In short, with students, your headaches typically won't be with evictions and late payments, but rather with higher expenses associated with the heavy wear and tear and high turnover rates. Your headaches may also come from the neighbors. It is a very unpopular landlord who rents a house to students in a neighborhood populated by predominantly owner-occupied dwellings.

Rooming Houses

I have included this section in order to differentiate rooming houses from standard apartment leases. In short, a rooming house exists when there are unrelated parties living together with *separate* leases. Unlike a typical lease that applies to the entire apartment unit, in a boarding house, the kitchen, living room, bathrooms, parking areas, etc., can all become common areas. As common areas, they thus become the responsibility of the landlord. Often, these rooming houses require a license from the local authorities.

In lieu of these facts, here are the reasons I am against entering into this type of an agreement. Because of the extended common area, any damage done to this part of your property is difficult to collect on. This is certainly true if you use a management company, as they usually won't get in the middle of these conflicts. A gouge in the vinyl, a non-allowed pet, a stain in the carpet, and a punched-in wall will all be difficult to get repaired at a tenant's expense. Additionally, since there are multiple leases, turnover is high and roommates are constantly coming and going. Due to the high turnover coupled with the fact that these unrelated parties must share common areas, roommate fallouts are common. In fact, one bad egg in your rooming house can quickly lead to a mass exodus, leaving you with a fraction of the original rental income and a tenant you need to get rid of.

On a more positive note, boarding houses can be very profitable if you can get your arms around the management challenges. Your gross rents per building are higher in a boarding house, as you have more units under one roof. Whereas you may rent a four-bedroom house to a family for $900 per month, in a boarding situation, you may get $300 per bedroom, or $1,200 per month. If you are willing to take on these high-management situations, and write leases to cover all eventualities, then they can be successful endeavors. Before you purchase such a property, be sure and check with the local authorities and understand what type of license is required.

Building Styles

Whether single-family, multifamily, townhouses, or condominiums, the layout and style of the building you buy is extremely important. You may like the price, and it may currently be rented and have a good cash flow, but you may find that no tenants remain past the initial lease term due to some negative property feature you over-looked. These features can be obvious, like basement apartments with no windows or the absence of off-street parking. They can also be much more subtle, like smaller room sizes or the lack of bath-rooms for roommate situations. Before you buy you must think like a tenant and consider all possibilities that could adversely affect its appeal as an apartment. Be especially alert to such problems when inspecting buildings that are empty or where all the tenants are new.

I once inspected a quadraplex that appeared to be a great deal. What was particularly confusing was that all the units were rent-ready but were vacant and not being advertised. When I asked where the tenants were, I was told the owner just didn't want to deal with management anymore so the units were left vacant. Being the eternal skeptic that I am, I eventually figured it out. After questioning the neighbors, I learned that every time it rained the backyard filled up with water. Sure enough, upon closer inspection I was able to discover a water line at the one-foot mark! The seller obviously made sure the tenants were vacated before trying to sell the place. In this way he did not need to disclose this information to any potential buyers. The following is another example of where subtle property features can dramatically affect profitability. We bought a house in a student area. Since the house had three bedrooms our cash flow calculations were based upon three students paying rent. We overlooked one critical feature—one of the bedrooms was unusually small. As one group of students after another paraded through the house, no one wanted to be the one stuck with the small bedroom. The result is that we currently own a three-bedroom house that rents as a two-bedroom and thus has a negative cash flow. In the following sections we will cover the basics of which buildings' attributes make the best investments and why.

Single Level, Two Story, Side-by-Side, and Over-Under Flats

Whether the apartments in the building you are considering purchasing are attached, detached, on a single level, side by side, or over-under will define the amount of rent you will be able to command. In short, all these property features can be grouped under what I would call *privacy considerations*. These attributes are important and should rank extremely high when evaluating different structure types to buy. All things being equal, a detached dwelling will rent better and command higher rents than attached units.

Single-family homes and duplexes will therefore rent for more than triplexes and quadraplexes, which should rent for more than small apartment buildings, garden apartments, or high-rise buildings.[8] Single-story living is preferred over multiple-story living, and units attached side by side are preferred over so-called flats that are over-under arrangements.

As we have seen previously, single-family homes are usually not a good investment. Your best bet therefore is to purchase a multi-family building that has single-family attributes and feel. Some examples of applying this rule are as follows. All things being equal, a duplex with side-by-side units is worth more and will rent better than an over-under duplex. A quadraplex that is a single level in a horse-shoe layout, with private entrances and yards, will command more rent per unit than a two-story, box-shaped complex with two flats up and two flats down.

Although these are all good rules of thumb, it is important that you understand what is important to your tenants in the area you wish to invest in. A swimming pool or fenced yard, for example, may make the difference between always having vacant units and keeping them filled.

Utilities, Bathrooms, and Parking

One of the most important features of any property you propose to buy is whether the utility hookups are paid by the landlord or are separate and therefore tenant-paid. Although it is rarely cost effective to achieve this in larger apartment buildings, smaller apartment buildings should have separate water, sewer, heating, and cooling bills. If there are any common utilities, for example, water, the owner usually must pay these bills. This can cut deeply into profits, especially when the tenants know the utility cost doesn't come out of their pocket. If you insist on going forward with a property where utilities are owner-paid, be sure to research the historical utility bills so you are not surprised when consumption doubles from one month to the next. This extra $100 per month, or whatever the expense, may be the only difference between a positive and negative cash flow.

The number of bathrooms per unit is important to today's renter. Apartments that have too few bathrooms are difficult to rent, especially if you are targeting a roommate situation. I have a duplex with two bedrooms and one bath per side. Due to the absence of the second bath we are missing out on a huge segment of the tenant population, namely young professionals who wish to live as roommates and want their own bathroom. For student rentals this feature is essential. These days it is common that student rentals have one bath per bedroom so each student has his or her own bath.

Another obvious feature that is important is the availability of parking. If you are buying in a downtown area where parking on the street is limited, be sure to ensure there are enough parking spaces for each unit. This especially applies for student areas. Figure in at least one and one-half spaces per bedroom (worst-case scenario) for student housing and one space per bedroom for non-student rentals.

Converting Single-Family to Multifamily

If you have an inclination toward building things, a very lucrative area of investing is converting single-family homes to multifamily structures. These opportunities exist when zoning laws allow multiple units where a single-family house stands. In general, such conversions are based upon the *best and highest utilization rules*. In short, this means that you get the most value out of a property when you utilize it in the highest level of allowed zoning use. If a single-family home is sitting on a lot that will permit a five-unit apartment building, the lot is being underutilized.

Neighborhoods that offer these conversion opportunities are easy to identify. Look for old, established neighborhoods where multifamily housing is mixed in with single-family properties. Look for construction or evidence that conversions have already been made. Then check the tax records to verify the zoning in that area. Become familiar with the building codes so you understand the rules and can readily identify building lots that would permit multifamily buildings. Once you have identified a potential neighborhood to invest in, you can monitor that area on Realtor.com. If a house comes up you can cross-reference it to the tax records to find out its zoning, or just call the realtor. Only consider adding on to an existing dwelling that has been updated recently. If you connect to an older building you may be required to update the services in the existing dwelling to current code standards. This additional cost will nearly always offset any gains achieved by adding on the new units.

In order to analyze these conversion projects, one needs to price out the value of equivalent properties in the area. Then, based upon local building costs per square foot, you can estimate the total cost for your conversion. Be sure not to exceed four units unless you are prepared to obtain commercial financing, which is typically required for five units and higher. Another consideration is that building codes will vary greatly depending on the number of units you propose to build. Duplexes, for example, may be considered residential, and therefore not subject to commercial building requirements such as handicap access and additional parking. A triplex, however, may be considered commercial and require such measures.

A final word of caution. These construction projects are high-risk and should be reserved for investors with ample experience buying, renovating, and renting property. A six-month vacancy period, or an unplanned $10,000 parking lot required by the city, can quickly put you into financial peril. My recommendation is to start out small. Become familiar with the building process and local building and zoning codes by adding on a single-bedroom unit or a two-bedroom unit. After this you can feel more comfortable committing to a larger job.

Occasionally it is tempting not to add on to a house but rather to divide a house into separate units. This approach, however, is rarely profitable unless you can convert it into at least several units. Having to separate utilities and bring everything up to code often makes this kind of project more costly than adding on to an existing structure. As a final word of advice for all these conversion projects, make sure that what you create has a look and feel of a conventional multi-housing structure. Pay attention to detail and ensure the entrances and living areas are private so that your new units are appealing to tenants at a competitive rent.

A unique advantage of these types of projects is that you often end up with a rental property that is completely updated and brand new. Because of its effective age, your expenses for the next several years will be very low. For this reason, new construction or renovations are attractive. We typically receive *no* service calls from these units, even after five years. Compared with your older units, these newer properties will typically add a minimum of an additional $100 per unit per month in profits.

The other advantage with this type of venture is that it is perfectly amenable to a no-money-down scheme. Initially, you must finance the construction either with cash or by using a construction loan. The construction loan is typically based upon a variable interest rate and is linked to the prime rate. They usually carry an initial term of six months. After your renovations are complete and you have all your units rented, you can usually refinance your project and exchange the construction loan for long-term conventional financing. If you organize things right, you can usually walk away from the closing table with no net money down on your new investment. The reason this works is that the appraised value of the improved building is usually higher than the cash you have invested into the project (providing your market value analysis was accurate). This value-added benefit is another reason why these projects can be very profitable. Regarding the timing of refinancing, you should realize that there is usually a six-month *seasoning* requirement by Fannie Mae on residential conventional financing. This essentially means that if you try and refinance prior to six months from the purchase date, the appraiser will be required to use the original sale price to determine value, not other value-indicating methods like the income approach or comparable sales approach. In short, you need to be prepared to wait at least six months before completing your project and finalizing your financing.

New Construction

If you have identified older multifamily-zoned neighborhoods you will undoubtedly also notice new construction opportunities in the form of teardowns and vacant lots. Such opportunities are worth investigating. As we previously mentioned, the investor gets great value from new construction due to the savings on repair and maintenance bills when compared to owning older properties. Often the owner can sell the property years later before any of the major repairs become due, adding to your bottom line profit.

In deciding what to build, the building code for duplex structures is often in the same category as single-family homes and is thus easier to get approved. For construction purposes, anything larger than two units is typically treated as commercial and the zoning and building code requirements become more restrictive. Before you begin you will need to research your local building code and determine what is necessary for the type of housing you propose.

Modular Housing

If you decide to build new you should consider modular housing. Modular construction is different from manufactured home construction. Both types of homes are manufactured in factories and the sections are then transported to the building site and then joined together by local contractors. The difference is that modular construction meets all the same state and local building codes as a site-built home and therefore will appraise and appreciate the same as a site-built home. Manufactured homes meet only the federal Department of Housing and Urban Development (HUD) building code standards, not state or local building codes. Manufactured homes come with permanent-fixed steel frame chassis, and are more familiar to us as mobile homes or trailers. Since manufactured homes do not meet local building codes they typically will not appreciate in value over time. Whereas local zoning will nearly always allow modular homes, manufactured homes, or mobile homes, may have zoning restrictions.

To add to the confusion, within the modular housing industry there is both *on-frame* and *off-frame* modular construction (sometimes referred to as *on-rail* or *off-rail*). Both of these types of modulars conform to stick-built code but differ in the following way. The on-frame modulars are usually set on a foundation with the steel frame permanently in place, then tied down with cables fixed to concrete pilings, much like a mobile home. The off-frame modulars have no steel frame and the wood is bolted directly to the pre-built foundation, the same as a stick-built house. In general, regardless of the terminology, stay away from modular housing that remains fixed to any type of rail or steel frame. Although the on-frame modulars may conform to local building codes, banks and appraisers have not caught up with the trade and they value on-frame structures more like mobile homes rather than stick-built homes. To make things even more confusing, off-frame modulars are often brought to the job site on-frame. So don't be alarmed if you order an off-frame modular and it arrives on-frame with wheels. As long as the frame is not permanently fixed, and they use the frame only to transport the building to the job site, it is still considered an off-frame modular. The following points summarize the many advantages of going with modular construction instead of traditional on-site, stick-built homes.

- Modular housing can be used for one or multiple units and is in every way identical in quality to most site-built homes.

- Modular housing is ideal for investment property as many manufacturers offer standard packages for duplexes, triplexes, and multi-unit apartment configurations, allowing precise project costing.

- With modular housing, pre-approved building plans are readily available, thus the investor can submit plans and obtain approval before committing any money. With site-built projects, architects must be paid to draw plans and contractors must bid on the plans before submitting for approval.

- Modular homes are not constructed over periods of months, but rather weeks, and thus project time and financing for the investor is predictable.

- Modular homes are delivered complete with all plumbing, electrical, HVAC, roof with shingles, and drywall, everything already built to local building code. Even the appliances are in place.

- With modular homes you are rarely disappointed, as you know exactly what you are getting and you can usually walk through show room examples before buying.

- If you shop around, modular housing will always be cheaper than stick built.

- As long as it is consistent with the neighborhood, a modular property will appraise and appreciate the same as a site-built home.

- Modular construction is ideal for investment property as the typical box-shape look, while less preferable for single-family structures, fits with multifamily construction styles. Additionally, many companies offer features that break up the box look should the investor wish to spend the extra money.

Although unlikely, before you begin your research into modular housing, be sure to check that there are no local zoning or community restrictions against this type of construction in your area. Additionally, to play it safe, be sure to contact several local appraisers and confirm that your proposed structure will appraise the same as a site-built property.

Summary

- In order to retain tenants, your rents should be below the cost of an entry-level mortgage payment for similar housing in your area.

- Multifamily properties typically provide more cash flow than single-family properties due to the unit discount associated with buying multi-unit apartments.

- Condos and townhomes may offer higher cash flow, but they are poorer investments because you own no land and homeowner dues are variable and can increase without notice.

- Apartment features that offer the tenant the most privacy will bring the highest rents.

- Renting to students can provide a reliable source of rental income but requires a high level of management.

- New construction offers great value for the investor as your maintenance and repair expenses are low and you can sell before all the repairs and maintenance expenses come due.

- Modular housing offers the same quality as stick-built homes for a very affordable *turn-key price*.

CHOOSING A LOCATION 5

Will Rogers once said that making money in real estate is simple, "all you have to do is go to where people are going to go before they go there and buy the land so that when they get there, you can sell it to them." That, by the way, is only half of his advice. The other half is, "if the people are not going to come, then don't buy the land." Demographics teach us *what* the future growth areas will be based upon—trends and need. Choosing *where* to invests however, requires a different set of criteria.

The Fundamentals

In order to realize your investment goals, you must purchase the right property in the right location. Identifying the right location to buy investment property is less obvious than deciding where to buy your own home. If you are looking to buy your own home, you may prefer areas where there are no renters at all. When you are choosing a location to invest in, however, you should target neighborhoods that are predominantly multifamily. These multifamily communities should have schools, public transportation, and retail and commercial businesses close by. These businesses provide the employment to your tenants. Avoid areas where there is only a single employer far and wide. Investing in these areas is high risk. If the local mill shuts down, your tenants will be gone along with the property values. Finally, the location of your property should be close to where you live or work. This will allow you to easily monitor the condition of your property.

In summary then, the ideal investment properties are:

- located in multifamily areas with a diverse job base

- located close to where you live or work

- located close to where your tenants will work

- located close to schools, public transportation, and recreation

Note that no mention of neighborhood quality has been made. Of course we would all like to have our investment property in the very best neighborhood, not unlike where we would live. The reality, however, is that property in such areas will rarely provide a positive cash flow. The real challenge then is finding areas to invest that offer the right attributes and yet are still capable of providing a cash flow.

Cash Flow versus Location

Although the most important rule of real estate investing is still "location, location, location," as an *investor,* one needs to be more thoughtful about the whole process. In deciding where to invest, you need to consider the critical drivers of successful investing such as cash flow, prospects for appreciation, and the level of management commitment required. We all know that every city has its upscale areas along with areas that can be classified as poverty areas with high crime and rundown housing. In addition to these more extreme ends of the spectrum, there is usually the middle to lower-income areas. As we will see, there is a direct relationship between property value (price), cash flow, appreciation potential, location, and risk. These relationships can be summarized as follows.

- High-priced areas are low-risk investments and have higher rates of appreciation, but typically offer negative cash flows.

- Low-priced areas have higher-risk, lower-appreciation potential, but typically offer high-cash flows.

- Medium-priced areas are in neither the best nor the worst neighborhoods, and provide both appreciation potential and cash flow.

So where should the private investor concentrate his or her efforts? Although we would love to buy in the security of steadily appreciating single-family, owner-occupied neighborhoods, these properties typically will *not* provide a positive cash flow. The best areas to buy are the low to mid-income areas, where property prices are also low to midrange. In other words, one needs to strike a *balance* between optimizing location *and* cash flow. As we have seen in our demographic studies, this low- to mid-income renter also comprises the largest segment of the rental market. In short, we want to target the areas where the tenants rent out of necessity, not choice. These tenants will tend to be long-term and will be a reliable source of income.

So how do we recognize these optimal areas to invest? These low to mid-income areas tend to be higher-density, mixed-use districts characterized by the presence of strip malls, hospitals, retail stores, offices, light-industrial businesses and other service industries, along with apartment housing. The providers of these services, such as teachers, nurses, police, administrative personnel, supermarket employees, office workers, and restaurant and retail staff, are the tenants you will rent to. In short, the apartments that are close to where your prospective tenants will work are your best investments.

Ideally, your target investment area should have well-kept, owner-occupied neighborhoods adjacent or nearby. There should be no evidence of widespread unemployment or drug activity as indicated by the presence of tenants loitering or walking the streets during normal business hours. The neighborhoods should be largely vacant by mid-morning as everyone is at work (verify this). There should not be widespread vacancy and the vacancy rate in your target area should not exceed local averages. No abandoned vehicles or boarded-up properties should be present or nearby.

Once you have identified your target area you must determine in what direction property values are heading. The area you propose to invest in should be an area that is appreciating in value, not depreciating. Appreciation values may be less than those typically seen for higher-income, owner-occupied neighborhoods, but the trend should still be upward. We will go into more detail in Chapter 7 on how to value properties and determine if areas are appreciating. These techniques should be used when evaluating potential target neighborhoods to invest in. One can—and must—verify this historical upward trend in appreciation before buying.

> **NOTE:**
> Interestingly, the notion that multifamily units located close to single-family homes decrease the property values of single-family homes seems largely unsubstantiated. In fact, one study found that between 1987 and 1995 single-family homes located within 300 feet of multifamily buildings appreciated just one-tenth of a percent less than the 3.2% appreciation seen among single-family homes without multifamily structures nearby.[9]

In summary, it is the high-density service corridors of a metropolitan area that provide the best balance between maximizing cash flow without compromising on location. These areas will still appreciate over time while providing a good cash flow with minimal risk of depreciation.

A particularly useful tool for identifying these low- to medium-income areas is to use a technique I call gross rent multiplier (GRM) screening.

Choosing Location Using GRMs

The gross rent multiplier (GRM) is simply the relationship between gross rents and sale price, as shown below.

$$GRM = \frac{Price}{Rent}$$

The GRM is the most popular income approach method of predicting real estate value for residential rental property, probably because it is easiest to understand. The GRM can be calculated using either yearly or monthly rents and both are commonly seen. Be careful of this distinction as there is a big difference between the two methods. A duplex, for example, with a sale price of $170,000 and gross rents of $1,400 per month or $16,800 per year can have two different GRMs depending on how they are calculated:

GRM Calculated Based Upon Monthly Gross Rents

$$GRM = \frac{\$170,000}{\$1,400} = 121$$

GRM Calculated Based Upon Yearly Gross Rents

$$GRM = \frac{\$170,000}{\$16,800} = 10$$

For the purposes of this exercise, it doesn't matter which method you use so long as you are consistent. I like to use the monthly income approach because you don't need to use fractions and it is based upon 100. As we can see from the above GRM equation, when price is high and rents are low, GRMs are high (Price↑, Rent↓; GRM↑). When price is low and rents are high, low GRMs result (Price↓, Rent↑; GRM↓). In terms of GRMs, one can thus make the following statements:

- *Low* GRM areas (low price + high rent) usually have *higher risk* and lower likelihood of appreciation. Your lowest GRMs are often found in the low-income, high-crime, and affordable-housing areas.

- *High* GRM areas (high price + low rent) are *lower risk* and are typically found in the more established, higher-income neighborhoods where appreciation has been high.

This GRM relationship between rental income and property value can be used to screen geographical areas and locate the preferred low- to mid-price range investment areas. If you calculate GRMs from different parts of your metropolitan area, a general trend should emerge. The method is simple. Just go to your local MLS website and begin by entering in zip codes and/or geographic areas (N, S, E, W). Then calculate the GRMs using the sale prices and listed rents. If you do this, clear patterns will emerge indicating low GRM areas, high GRM areas, and mid-GRM areas. What we are looking for is to stay away from the extreme ends of the spectrum and target the low- to mid-range GRM areas. These are the areas that will represent the best balance between profit and risk. The following tables were generated using this technique and are based on actual data taken from the MLS in a large metropolitan area in the United States.

Whatcom firm:
282

Calculated GRMs for *Anytown, USA**

Location 1: SE Central; *Average GRM = 60*

Property Type	Gross Monthly Rents	Listing Price	GRM
2 units	$695	$38,700	56
2 units	$750	$55,000	73
4 units	$1,380	$70,000	51

*Rents are actual market rents. Properties are of similar age.

Location 2: Central; *Average GRM = 185*

Property Type	Gross Monthly Rents	Listing Price	GRM
2 units	$1,300	$269,000	206
4 units	$2,200	$330,000	150
2 units	$1,100	$220,000	200

Location 3: SW Central; *Average GRM = 129*

Property Type	Gross Monthly Rents	Listing Price	GRM
4 units	$2,000	$250,000	125
2 units	$1,100	$165,000	150
4 units	$2,300	$260,000	113

Location 4: NW Central; *Average GRM = 130*

Property Type	Gross Monthly Rents	Listing Price	GRM
2 units	$1,300	$180,000	138
2 units	$1,400	$190,000	136
2 units	$1,350	$160,000	118

The first thing you notice by performing this analysis is that it is only part science. The age, condition, and whether units are vacant or not all affect price, and therefore GRMs. Also, asking price does not equal selling price, so GRMs that are based upon asking price would be expected to be inflated.

Despite these shortcomings, in general, *patterns* should emerge based upon neighborhoods (target areas of investment). It is important that you determine these patterns. As mentioned previously, stay away from the *very low* and *very high* GRMs. The midrange GRMs should provide the best balance between optimizing cash flow without sacrificing appreciation potential. These mid- to low-GRM areas should also be areas that are consistent with our previous socioeconomic analysis. In the current case study this would correspond to Locations 3 and 4, where GRMs range from 113 to 150.

Another important rule when doing this type of analysis is to be sure and group properties by similar number of units. There is always a *cost per unit* discount for properties with multiple units, so your GRM should be specific to the number of units. In fact, if you look at these random samplings, you can note a trend that four-unit buildings are discounted (lower GRMs) compared to the two-unit buildings. This particular study was targeting the two to four unit (small apartment) properties. If you are interested in larger apartment buildings, you would need to restrict your GRM screening to the appropriate building types.

Although this analysis will vary somewhat depending on your geographic location, we will go on to show that a monthly GRM of less than 115 should provide a positive cash flow, assuming a 30-year mortgage at 6% and 20% down (80% LTV). Thus in addition to choosing a mid-range GRM, *ideally* you should end up at a GRM of less than 115 to ensure a positive cash flow. We will provide more exact tools for calculating whether the property will have a positive cash flow or not, but this general rule of thumb should hold up.

> **NOTE:**
> Although using GRMs to predict cash flow provides a good "benchmark," you should always verify cash flow by calculations based upon current available interest rates and property specifics as described in Chapter 6.

PCF = L 115 GRM

GRM Summary

- Low GRM areas have higher cash flows than high GRM areas but have lower potential of appreciation (higher risk of depreciation).

- High GRM areas produce lower cash flows but have greater probability of a high appreciation rate.

- Mid-GRM areas are the best balance in order to achieve a positive cash flow and still have a good probability of appreciation.

- All things being equal (same socioeconomic area), GRMs will go down, and thus cash flow up, as you increase the number of units per lot.

- A general rule-of-thumb for small apartment buildings is that a monthly GRM of less than 115 *should* provide a positive cash flow based upon a 20% down payment with a 6% interest rate and 30-year fixed-rate mortgage.

Suburban Sprawl

Investing in multifamily properties that are located in high-density, mixed-use service sector areas is preferred on yet another level; namely, it is these areas that are predicted to be the high-growth areas of the future. Over the last century, the U.S. population has steadily moved from urban areas to the suburban periphery. After the Second World War, the federal government supported such growth with the GI Bill and the promotion of the Federal Highway Act. Now, fifty years later, suburban growth has become a problem, as is exemplified by metropolitan areas such as Atlanta, Georgia. Atlanta, at the time of this writing, is now estimated to span over 110 miles from end to end. This resulting *sprawl* can be found in every metropolitan area in the United States and has created traffic congestion, pollution, and the expansion of urban blight from inner cities to inner suburbs. As people increasingly turn their attention to these issues, the so-called *smart growth* utilization of multifamily development is becoming more commonplace in city planning throughout the country. Increasingly, local and federal agencies are "rethinking" the suburban development approach to city planning. It is likely these trends will continue. The development of so-called *edge cities*—employment centers outside of city centers and surrounded by suburban development—is becoming more common.

Affordable multifamily housing makes it possible for moderate- to low-income wage earners—the service sector referred to previously—to live in these edge cities and provide the services we depend on from our suburban retreats.

For these reasons and those cited previously, the smart investor should be targeting these *mixed-use* areas to invest in. The biggest risk we face, as fortune tellers in this game, is whether the urban blight from inner cities will spread outward and ultimately bring down property values in these fringe areas where we invest. For this reason, you must pay very close attention to socioeconomic trends within the areas you propose to, or already have, invested in. Increased crime could be a signal that property depreciation is imminent. Follow your appreciation rates yearly. As soon as a downward trend becomes apparent in conjunction with these other symptoms, it is time to sell.

Main Street or Dead-End Streets?

Having established a suitable geographical area to invest in based upon GRMs and socioeconomic considerations, one needs to consider local topography. In general, homeowners prefer the privacy of dead-end streets, cul-de-sacs, and houses on a hill—the *privacy considerations* discussed earlier. Tenants are no different. Given the choice, they also prefer remote, secluded housing. Such remote areas, however, are *not* desirable from an investor's standpoint on several levels. You or your tenant may like the idea of living on a nice, private dead-end street or cul-de-sac but consider this. I once looked at eleven units for sale right on a busy four-lane thoroughfare. I thought, "No way would I buy here. I would rather live in a nice quiet area, and thus that must be true for the tenants as well." The older, more seasoned investor who was selling the properties said, "Great location, right on the bus line, and they rent quickly with only a sign posted out front due to the high traffic exposure." Years later I realized he was right—but only after paying $600 in classified ads and $200 for utilities on a three month vacancy because the property we owned was buried deep in a neighborhood. The take-home lesson is this: buy properties with good street exposure, and beware of properties that are located six turns into a neighborhood. With most cities up in arms against posting signs, you won't be able to get enough pointer signs to lead the tenants to your units. Interestingly enough, most renters find their new apartments by driving in the areas they want to live, thus the importance of this subtle location feature.

The local police might also add that remote, less accessible areas are a magnet for drugs and crime and in fact are usually the seed areas that bring down neighborhoods. As a landlord and investor, you certainly don't want to be the one leading that trend.

Student Housing

The location considerations governing your selection of student housings will be based upon an entirely different set of criteria. There is no need to think very hard about where to invest. If you wish to target the student housing market there is only one correct answer—the closer to the university the better. If you *cannot* walk or take the bus to the university from the property you are considering, then you need to be the one doing the walking. Any remote housing for students is too vulnerable to the next new student housing facility with a bathroom for every room and free drinks in the lounge every evening at happy hour. The point is, you can't keep up with student preferences in housing trends so don't try. Ten years ago, having one bath for every two bedrooms was the benchmark for student rentals. Today, each student wants, in fact expects, to have his or her own bathroom. If you can't offer the newest and best—and you can never keep up with this—then you must have an attribute that will survive time eternal, namely location. Properties that are within walking distance of the university are prized and in limited supply, much like beach property. I have seen old dilapidated houses rent like hot cakes because they sit right on the university campus. These same houses would sit vacant if they were but a mile farther away from the university. Housing located on the student bus line comes next in preference. You have to use your judgment as each city and each university is different. I usually evaluate whether it is a good student area by taking a quick survey of the ratio of students to non-students in the area. You definitely want to be in a neighborhood that is dominated by students. A few single-family homeowners can spoil your investment if they are adverse to students living next door. Definitely stay away from single-family, owner-occupied neighborhoods near a university. It will only be a matter of time before the neighborhood organizes, your student rental becomes a target of public ridicule, and your student tenants move on.

Appreciation and Growth Trends

We have talked in general terms about the desirable factors to look for in a neighborhood and we have learned how to identify the most profitable areas by using GRMs. In addition to verifying historical appreciation trends, there are certain dynamic factors that can be used to identify growth patterns, demand, and thus appreciation. Before we address these factors, recall that there are two types of appreciation: appreciation due to inflation and appreciation due to supply and demand factors. *Inflationary appreciation* is simply the increase in the cost of building materials, building permits, and labor, all of which lead to an increase in the value of your brick and mortar over time. All landlords will benefit from this type of appreciation. The second type of appreciation is the *real appreciation,* or the appreciation of the land or location. For this type of appreciation, housing demand must exceed supply. Obviously the best opportunities to profit from are areas where the land is in short supply. Areas such as Manhattan and Hong Kong are common examples where geographical restrictions can lead to high property value appreciations. Here developers must raze existing buildings and build newer and higher buildings to achieve increasing value from the same piece of land. The supply and demand of housing can also be influenced through the action of local planning authorities. Most cities have master plans outlining how they see the city being developed. If your local authorities have a master growth plan, areas of growth and thus appreciation can be predicted. Look for areas where these plans are already being implemented and there are signs of positive changes, like the building of new transportation hubs, malls, museums, hospitals, or any type of development that would provide employment to your prospective tenants. If there is neither a geographical advantage, nor a well-organized plan for growth, predicting the likelihood of appreciation is more difficult. Often the direction of growth appears random as developers keep moving to more remote areas where the land is cheap. The previous example of suburban sprawl is a good example of this lack of planning. In these regions, property values may increase no more than the rate of inflation.

The following list summarizes some of the important dynamics that can affect supply and demand and thus property appreciation. None of these factors work alone and many are interrelated. As an investor, you should consider the effects of all these factors before making any decisions to invest.

- **Interest rates**. The availability of money and how much it costs can directly affect future values of real estate. As mortgage rates increase, the demand for real estate decreases and vice versa.

- **Building activity**. Increased building is a good sign as long as the building activity is diverse and includes retail and commercial as well as residential activity.

- **Location of the property**. Coastal properties have been increasing in value at a fast pace due to demand from the baby boomer population. Proximity to recreation such as golf courses, cultural facilities, parks, universities, and colleges can result in a higher rate of appreciation.

- **Local economy**. Changes in the infrastructure of an area can have a large impact on the demand for property. Increases in the infrastructure, for example in the service sectors discussed earlier, usually translate into more jobs and greater demand for real estate.

- **Population growth and patterns**. The demand for real estate in general has been increasing over time due to population increases. When this is coupled with reduced supply due to geographic or local planning constraints, the effect on appreciation can be dramatic.

- **Zoning**. Make sure you know what the zoning is in your target area of investment and whether it fits in with the city's future master plan. Consider other factors such as road infrastructure. Is the property's road frontage likely to be expanded or stay the same? Local planning commissions can usually supply answers to these questions.

- **New housing starts**. If the level of new housing starts in a particular area of the country is high, home prices will likely be increasing. To understand the long-term picture, the investor should determine what is driving the demand (if anything) and if it will continue.

- **Crime and safety**. The safety of a neighborhood can affect housing demand. As investors, you should not invest in an area where crime is high or trending upwards. If you don't feel safe walking around at night, neither will your tenants.

As a real estate investor, you should be looking for a combination of the aforementioned factors that will result in a high level of future appreciation. Unfortunately, choosing the right location is more art than science. Despite all the research you may do, you will still miss your mark occasionally. If your target property cash flows and the demographics fit, you have done all that you can. If you buy and hold for the long term, you are not likely to lose. Real estate values generally go up in the long run, with few exceptions.

CAUTION:
As a final word of advice, if you need to consider investing in a high-risk area to achieve affordable cash flows, be careful. You may bet that a high-crime area will turn around and you will retire rich ahead of schedule, but don't count on it. In just about every city we can find neighborhoods that have been boarded up for more years than you want to wait. In these cases it is important to do your homework and wait until you see some signs of positive infrastructure changes, such as teardowns and increased building activity.

Investing in High-Priced Markets

We have provided the formula to locate properties and we suggest a target GRM of 115 to achieve a break-even cash flow. Unfortunately, in many areas of the country it may not be possible to find such properties. A good measure of the availability of affordable housing for the investor is the ratio of house prices to yearly rental income, the so-called "house price to rent ratio." Although applied to owner-occupied housing, this ratio is not unlike the gross rent multiplier (GRM) when calculated based upon yearly rental income.

$$\text{House price to rent ratio} = \frac{\text{House Price}}{\text{Yearly Rental Income}}$$

This ratio can be viewed as the real estate equivalent of a stock's price-earnings ratio. Rapid increases of home prices combined with a flat rental market lead to high house price to rent ratios and can signal the onset of a bubble. In the United States, the ratio of house price to rents over the years for both single-family dwellings and larger rental structures has averaged between 11 and 12. If we convert our target GRM of 115 to yearly rents, we obtain a (rounded) house price to rent ratio of 10, which is close to historical levels. At the time of this writing, the current national house price to rent ratio has steeply increased and is now up to 17. In many of the hottest markets, such as in California, Florida, and New York, price to rent ratios have jumped to 20 to 30. These price levels are about two to three times higher than what you would need to have a positive cash flow property assuming a typical down payment at current interest rates. Interestingly, the price to rent ratios in many areas of the United States has remained unchanged. The data for your area is readily available through the NAR or by performing an Internet key word search. Although market timing should be less important for the long-term investor, if you are investing in one of these high price to rent areas, the possibility of a housing market correction is very real. Some of these corrections could take ten or more years to return to their original levels. What should you do if you live in such an area and you want to invest in rental property? Unfortunately, you do not have many options. You can expand your geographic target area until you find the higher cash flow properties. You can move into the higher-risk, higher-crime neighborhoods where cash flows are higher. You can try to buy larger apartment buildings with more units to take advantage of the per unit discount. You can buy foreclosures or rehab units so you can add value back into the property. If you own real estate, you may consider selling your existing property and moving the equity into an income-producing property. A combination of these efforts, along with an interest-only loan and a higher down payment, can go a long way toward making a property profitable, especially if you are the "on-site" manager to keep maintenance and repair charges down.

3/08: WHATCOM
23x

Summary

- High-priced housing areas are low-risk investments and have higher appreciation potential but rarely offer a positive cash flow.

- Low-priced housing areas are higher risk and have lower appreciation potential, but typically offer higher cash flow potential.

- The best areas to invest that maximize both cash flow and appreciation potential are in the low- to mid-priced "mixed use" areas.

- GRMs can be used as a screening tool to identify the best areas to invest; neither the very high nor the very low GRM areas are preferred, but it is rather the low- to mid-range GRMs that offer the best opportunity for cash flow and appreciation.

- Follow the appreciation trends of your investments periodically—as soon as a downward trend becomes apparent, consider selling.

- Avoid remote dead-end streets or cul-de-sacs when buying rental property, as such areas offer no advertising exposure and are difficult to rent, and are also magnets for drug and crime activity.

- When investing in student rental property, the best investments are those that are within walking distance to the university.

- Finding properties that will have a positive cash flow in a high house price to rent area is challenging and these areas are more likely to see a market correction.

DETERMINING CASH FLOW

6

When deciding whether you should buy a particular rental property, you need to be concerned with three things in the following priority. First, you will need to ensure you have a positive cash flow. Second, you should not pay more than fair market value for your property, and third, your investment must increase in value over time. Many investors are willing to settle for a negative cash flow in the hopes of selling someday for big capital gains. This is a poor investment decision. You may end up owning property that has a negative cash flow, but you shouldn't knowingly enter into such an agreement. After all, as we have seen from the POMS survey in Chapter 1, the number one reason why investors buy and hold on to rental property is for the income. Unfortunately though, we also learned that nearly half of those property owners were losing money on their investments. We also learned that the owners of single-family homes and small apartment buildings (1–4 units) were losing the most. Why, then, are so many private investors burdened with negative cash flows? Although neighborhoods can deteriorate and turn positive cash flow properties into negative flow investments, this is rarely the reason for negative cash flow earnings. The primary reason for negative cash flows is that the buyers of these properties used the wrong assumptions when they estimated cash flow. The two elements of cash flow are rental income and operating expenses. It is these two components that we need to get right before we can accurately project cash flow. If we buy a property that is renting for $800 per unit but later discover the actual *market* rents are closer to $750, we have made the wrong assumption. If we use a vacancy rate of 5% and the average vacancy for the area is closer to 10%, we have used the wrong assumption. If we don't factor in bathroom renovations or a replacement driveway in five years, our expense estimates are wrong. To summarize, the two common mistakes made by novice investors that lead to negative cash flows are:

1. The cost of operating expenses such as maintenance, repairs, and yearly cash reserves is *underestimated*.

2. The projected income from rents is *overestimated*.

In order to buy profitable properties it is essential you get your assumptions correct. If you miss your mark, you too will join the ranks of owners who lose money. The main focus of this chapter is to provide you with the tools to *precisely* predict expenses and market rents. With this data in hand, calculating cash flow is simple. Follow these basic rules and you should become a member of the property owners that are profitable, and be well on your way to building wealth through investing in real estate.

Myth versus Reality

Pick up nearly any book on investing in real estate and the *rule of thumb*, or example used, is that a house that sells for $100,000 should rent for $1,000 per month. This 10% rule, or 100 gross rent multiplier rule, still dominates the investment literature. Unfortunately, such properties are becoming increasingly hard to find. Why does this myth persist then? The rule perpetuates because every investor knows that *those* properties *will* be profitable. If there were an abundance of such properties, the number of profitable owners of small apartments would be greater than the 40% we found in the POMS study. Unfortunately, that is not the case. In fact, higher property values coupled with lower rents over the years make it increasingly more difficult to find such *high cash flow properties*. One *can* find properties that hold up to this 10% rule; however, they will not be in prime locations but will more likely be located in high-crime, high-risk areas. For these properties, the large cash flows are often offset by high vacancies, defaults in rent, high management costs, and the risk of *property depreciation* over time. Unless you want to own property in these types of neighborhoods, you will need to *lower* your expectations on cash flow. In short, we need to dispel the myth, and move on to reality.

We will therefore need to develop *new* standards that apply to our current investment market. So if a gross rent multiplier of ten times monthly rent is an impossible goal, then what number is the more realistic multiplier? What should our new standard of profitability be? More importantly, how can we ensure a profitable operation when investing in a single-family home, duplex, triplex, quadraplex, or apartment building? The following sections will provide answers to these questions.

Determining Operating Expenses

In order to calculate profitability and cash flow accurately on your rental properties, it is imperative you have a reliable way to predict your expenses. Predictable (fixed) expenses such as your mortgage, taxes, insurance, and homeowners' fees are easy to get right. Granted, all of these can go up, but for the most part, there shouldn't be huge surprises here. Variable expenses, however, such as maintenance, repairs, and capital improvement expenses, are more difficult to forecast. These expenses will largely be determined by the age, type, and size of the apartment building, and also by the extent maintenance has been deferred. As a result of the POMS study referred to earlier, we have some excellent guidance on what we can expect to pay per unit on operating expenses. The following discussion summarizes the study's findings.

The first study presents data on the median yearly operating costs paid per unit by the 16,000 participating property owners. Total operating expenses is defined as including *all* expenses except mortgage debt. The data is presented both in absolute dollar cost as well as a percent of gross rental income. The study queried both small and large property owners. This data is summarized in the table below.

Total Operating Costs Per Unit	Total	1–4 Units	5–49 Units	>50 Units
Costs per unit*	$2,300	$2,300	$2,600	$3,300
Costs as a percent	42.5%	42.5%	43.3%	50.0%

Yearly Total Operating Expenses by Unit

Source: "Property Owners and Managers Survey (POMS)" by U.S. Census 2000.
**Percentages were calculated using rent data reported in the POMS survey. For additional information on how this data was determined, see Appendix A.*

Overall, total operating expenses per unit ranged from a low of 42% to a high of 50%, when reported as a percentage of gross rental income. Expenses increased with the number of units in the apartment. Small apartments (1–4 units) had expenses totaling approximately 42.5% of gross rents, medium-sized apartments (5–49 units) had expenses of 43.3%, and large apartment complexes (>50 units) had expenses totaling approximately 50% of gross rents. The trend of increasing expenses with apartment size is not surprising. Large apartment buildings have more common areas to maintain and typically offer community amenities, all of which contribute to an increase in expenses.

The next study we will look at presents data on the repair and maintenance expenses paid per unit. For this expense, which is a subset of total operating expenses, the costs as a percentage of gross rents ranged from a low of 14% for small properties to a high of about 18% for medium and large properties. The actual distribution for maintenance repair costs as a function of unit size is shown in the figure below:

Yearly Total Maintenance Expenses by Unit

Maintenance Costs	Total	1–4 Units	5–49 Units	>50 Units
Costs as a percent of rental income	14.0%	14.0%	18.0%	18.0%

Source: "Property Owners and Managers Survey" by U.S. Census 2000.

As was observed with the total operating expense data presented previously, the cost of maintenance and repairs is also found to increase uniformly with the size of the apartment building.

As we will discover in the following sections, this expense data, when combined with accurate market rent determinations, will allow us to accurately predict cash flows for rental properties.

Calculating Cash Flow

We have talked in general terms about cash flow, but let's now look into how cash flows are actually calculated. The definition of cash flow is simply the money you have left after you have collected all your rents and paid all your expenses. The formula for cash flow can be presented as follows:

$$\begin{array}{r} \text{Net Operating Income} \\ - \text{ Total Annual Debt} \\ \hline \text{Cash Flow} \end{array}$$

Total annual debt (TAD) would be your annual loan payments in the form of principal and interest. Net operating income (NOI) is simply the cash you have left after you have collected your rental income and paid all your expenses. NOI can be defined as follows:

$$
\begin{array}{r}
\text{Gross Rental Income} \\
-\ \text{Vacancy Rate} \\
\underline{-\ \text{Total Operating Expenses}} \\
\text{Net Operating Income}
\end{array}
$$

Clearly, when we consider our cash flow equation, we want our net operating income, or NOI, to be sufficient to cover our total annual debt, or TAD. The following simple relationship can be established between NOI and TAD:

$$
\begin{array}{l}
\text{If } NOI > TAD \text{ then } \textit{Positive Cash Flow} \\
\text{If } NOI = TAD \text{ then } \textit{``Break-even'' Cash Flow} \\
\text{If } NOI < TAD \text{ then } \textit{Negative Cash Flow}
\end{array}
$$

Note that the cash flow calculations cover the entire debt, which includes the principal payments as well. If your NOI is sufficient to cover your debt, you may have a zero cash flow but you are building equity by mortgage-pay down.

Let's combine these concepts and look at a typical cash flow estimation for a potential investment property. Consider the previous duplex example that was listed for sale at $160,000. For financing we will assume a 20% down payment so our loan amount will be $128,000. Assuming a 6% interest rate on a 30-year loan, our principal and interest payment would be $767.42 per month, or $9,209 per year. The advertised rent for this duplex is $700 per side, or $16,800 in gross rental income per year. We will assume a 5% vacancy rate. To estimate our projected expenses, items such as taxes, insurance, management fees, and utilities are usually available either from tax records, the seller, or other sources. For maintenance and repair we will use an estimate of 15% of gross rental income, which is based upon the values reported in the POMS survey. Combining all this information, we can now calculate cash flow as follows:

EXAMPLE:

Cash Flow Calculation for a Duplex

Address:	1002 Landlord Lane
Sale Price:	$160,000
Building Type:	2 units

Financing: 20% down on a 30-year fixed-rate loan at 6%

Market rent:	$700 per unit
Gross Rental Income	$16,800
Less 5% Vacancy	–$840
Net Rental Income	**$15,960**
Less Operating Expenses:	
Real Estate Taxes	$1,600
Insurance	$700
Repairs & Maintenance	$2,520
Utilities	$100
Management	$1176
Yearly Reserves	+ $1234
Total Operating Expenses	**$7,330**
Net Rental Income	$15,960
Less Total Operating Expenses	–$7,330
Net Operating Income (NOI)	**$8,630**
Less Total Annual Debt (TAD)	–$9,209
Cash Flow	**–$579**

NOTE:

Repairs and maintenance do not include capital expenditures, the so-called "reserves," such as the replacement of appliances, a roof, heating systems, or new carpet. The annualized cost estimate for these expenses is known as your "yearly reserves." Example calculations for yearly reserves can be found in Appendix B.

In this case we find that the net operating expenses (NOI) are less than the total annual debt (TAD). The property therefore has a slight negative cash flow of $579 per year.

In our previous example we were provided with all the operating expenses. Although the total operating expenses can vary greatly from property to property, it turns out that for most rental properties the total expenses can be approximated at 45% of gross rents. This expense factor assumes the units are in good condition and not in need of immediate repairs. If the dwelling in question is very old or very new then adjustments would need to be made. For most small apartment buildings, though, this value will provide a good benchmark to predict cash flows. With these assumptions, let's look at some examples that illustrate the use of this expense factor to predict cash flows. We will make the same assumptions as in our previous example, but now we will assign a value for total operating expenses of 45% of gross rental income:

> NOTE:
> A simple "rule of thumb" is that total operating expenses for small apartment buildings should be between 40% and 50% of the total gross rental income. Use of this expense factor should be limited to small apartment buildings of 1–5 units. For larger unit buildings a higher expense ratio may be necessary. For newer construction, a lower expense factor should be used. For more information on the assumptions that went into this expense factor, see Appendix A.
>
> Simplified Cash Flow Calculation
> **Address:**   1004 Landlord Lane
> **Sale Price:** $250,000
> **Building Type:**   4 units
> **Financing:** 20% down payment on a 30 year 6% fixed rate
> **Market rent:** $550 per unit

Total Operating Expenses: Assume 45% of gross rental income.	
Gross Rental Income	$26,400
Less Vacancy Rate (5%)	–$1,320
Net Rental Income	**$25,080**
Less Total Operating Expenses (45%)	–$11,880
Net Operating Income (NOI)	**$13,200**
Total Annual Debt (TAD)	–$14,389
Cash Flow	**–$1,189**

In this case, the yearly cash flow is estimated to be negative $1,189 per year. In order to make up this cash flow deficit, you would need to put more than 20% down, find better financing, or make a lower offer. This is where the fun comes in and where you can make the deal work by getting the seller to come down in price, obtaining better financing, or putting more money down to reduce your annual debt.

Effect of Interest Rates on Cash Flow

Using the previous example, if we are able to get a 5% interest rate instead of 6%, our yearly debt is reduced, and a slight positive cash flow is predicted.

Cash flow estimate for 1004 Landlord Lane at 5% interest rate

Net Operating Income	$13,200
– Total Annual Debt	–$12,883
Cash Flow	+$317

If you obtained a 5% *interest only* loan, your yearly debt would be $9,996 per year. Substituting into our DCR equation, one obtains a strong DCR ratio, even for bank standards, of 1.32 and a yearly positive cash flow of $3,200.

Cash flow estimate for 1004 Landlord Lane at 5% interest-only rate

Net Operating Income	$13,200
− Total Annual Debt	−$9,996
Cash Flow	+$3,204

Now you can see why interest-only loans are very popular. Just be aware that with interest-only loans no one is paying off your loan, thus your original loan amount will not be reduced over time.

The expense factor of 45% is useful for quickly screening profitability, but is a crude estimate nonetheless. If the units are new, or have been newly renovated, then the expense component would be less in the early years, maybe 30–40%. Another key point to remember is that this expense assumption *does not* include the cost of renovations, or replacing a driveway, removing trees, or putting up a fence. These costs would need to be considered as part of the sale in order to have a completely accurate cash flow prediction in the years to come. Once you have narrowed down your search to a few properties, you are encouraged to do exact calculations and break out all the expenses. As this is rather tedious without the aid of a computer, we recommend purchasing a simple software program to make these cash flow approximations (more on this later).

TIP: If you plan on managing the property yourself and handling the maintenance, total operating expenses can be as low as 20–30% of your gross rental income.

GRMs to Predict Cash Flow

Gross rent multipliers (GRMs) can be used to estimate cash flow potential. In the previous chapter we made a statement that a monthly GRM of less than 115 should provide positive cash flow, assuming certain financing conditions such as a 20% down payment and a 6%

interest rate. Since GRMs do not factor in the local vacancy rate, operating expenses, or the financing you may be getting, they are less precise. For example, if we calculate the GRM from our previous quadraplex example, we obtain the following:

Address:	1004 Landlord Lane
Sale Price:	$250,000
Market rent:	$550 per unit ($2,200 per month)

Recall that GRM is simply the ratio of sale price to gross rents. In the above case we obtain a GRM that is lower than 115, and would thus predict profitability.

$$GRM = \frac{Price}{Rent} = \frac{\$250,000}{\$2,200} = 114$$

As we have seen, however, when we use more accurate cash flow calculations and factor in the financing terms, this example property can range from profitable (at a 5% interest rate) to slightly unprofitable (at a 6% interest rate). For this reason the use of GRMs should be used only when a very crude estimate of cash flow potential is desired.

Cash Flow Calculators

Calculating cash flows assuming a 45% expense factor is a great way to screen properties for cash flow. Once you identify a potential property, however, you will want to perform more detailed cash flow calculations where you itemize all your expenses. A more accurate method of calculating cash flows makes use of one of the many *cash flow calculator* computer programs available. They are quite easy to use and provide accurate predictions of positive or negative cash flows. Like all computer calculations, they are only as accurate as your input data. This is where the data on maintenance and repair and yearly reserve data we provide in Appendix B are invaluable. Other expenses should be readily available from tax records, local utility companies, or the seller. Using this information, you can accurately predict these variable expenses that every buyer worries about getting right. With a firm grasp of your operating expenses, you can input the right numbers into these computer programs and get meaningful outputs. You may find however, that when you break down all your expenses, you will be quite close to the 45% expense factor you used initially! These programs are also useful because they automatically do all the amortization schedules (PI) for you. They also allow "sensitivity" calculations. For example, note that in the previous examples we *chose* a vacancy rate of 5%. This may be the current vacancy rate, but if vacancy rates went up to 10% for two years, would you be able to survive financially? These programs permit you to calculate these different sensitivity scenarios. One can purchase quite sophisticated programs for several hundred dollars, but for a fraction of the cost, one can obtain Microsoft Excel based versions that work quite well. Using these programs and the right data, your cash flow calculations should then be very close to being correct over the long term.

Determine the Market Rents

In order to obtain correct cash flow estimates, your projected income from rents must be accurate. A $25 per month error in rent on your part could mean the difference between a negative or positive cash flow. So let's consider the $700 per month rent we used in our previous duplex example. Where did that number come from? Is that the current rent? Are the units vacant and $700 is the market rent estimated by the seller's agent? In fact, none of these rent estimates should be used for your calculations. What we need to determine are the *actual* market rents for those units in that neighborhood. How do you accomplish this? You must perform a market analysis of rents for your property. Locate "For Rent" signs, and call and ask about rents. Find adjacent property owners in the county tax records and call them up. Tell them you are interested in investing in that neighborhood. Tell them right off you are a landlord. I have had 100% success rate doing this. One rarely hangs up on a fellow landlord. You will find most folks are quite up front about their rents. Some will say, "Oh, I have rented that unit for $575 to the same tenant for over nine years without raising the rent" (this is a *below market* data point). Another might say, "Well, I just renovated the place and it took me two months to get $725 for it." Now you have a good data point for an actual market rent. *Verify, verify, verify.* Do not trust any information you obtain from the seller or seller's agent at face value, even if it is based upon existing tenants. If you discover that the actual market rents are lower than $700 per unit, you can recalculate cash flow based upon the true market rents. You can then present a lower offer to the seller and explain why. Do not spend much time with the deal, however, if the seller isn't willing to come down in price. Just move on to the next deal. As a final note, remember that accurate cash flow calculations depend on accurate vacancy determinations. Recall that a convenient way to obtain the vacancy rate is by comparing the number of "For Rent" signs to the total number of mailboxes in the neighborhood.

Appreciation Makes Up for Negative Cash Flow

It always upsets me every time I read a new book on real estate investing and the assumptions are always the same. "Rents and property values *always* increase over time." As with many truths in investing, this is only partially right. As we have seen with the stock market recently, we can *no* longer make the claim that stocks will increase over *any* ten-year period. Real estate is no different. Although appreciation in property values may be more predictable than the stock market, rent appreciation is not. Nationally, median rents have increased over the last ten years. Although the national trend is upward, *local* rent trends can be quite different. In our metropolitan area for example, ten years ago, a two-bedroom, two-bath townhouse rented for $700 per month. Today, fifteen years later, that *same* unit still rents for $700. A three-bedroom student rental twenty years ago brought $850 per month in rent. Today, the same comparable units rent for $795. This rent depression affected all parts of our rental market, both the highly appreciating areas, as well as the poorer, less-appreciating areas. Although these rent depreciations are admittedly rare, to the affected investors these down cycles are very costly. We bought our very first rental property in a well-established suburban neighborhood. We paid $123,000 for our Manchester Drive house, a three-bedrooms two-bath home. We rented this house to start at $1,200 per month. Even a back of the envelope calculation would predict this to be profitable, and, in fact, it was in the beginning. In the following two years we managed to get $1,150, and then eventually it sat vacant for six months. Our top rent five years later? $925! Keep in mind this was a very nice house in a very upstanding neighborhood, and it remains so to this day. There are no multifamily properties and maybe only three or four rental properties in the whole subdivision. It turns out that during this period rents had precipitously fallen due to a glut of single-family homes. Everyone wanted to be a landlord and instead of people moving and selling, they moved and rented their homes. These novice landlords were largely uninformed and assumed if their rent covered their mortgage payment, then they were making money. This perception, along with increased supply, served to drive down rents to unprofitable levels. Such rent depression is not unique to our metropolitan area and is typically found in sprawling areas where land is readily available for development. Oddly, the National Association of Realtors (NAR) records for our area actually indicated that rents climbed during this period. They probably did, *on the average*, but not for older single-family homes which we happened to own. My point? Cash flows are extremely important. It is *critical* that your new purchase is profitable based upon today's dollars. If the numbers don't work in today's dollars, you may experience that negative cash flow for many years to come. If you own five such properties, it could ultimately cause your financial ruin. As you can see, even if the numbers are positive when you buy, you may still need to survive some hard times. The likelihood of success, however, is high when you start out with the correct assumptions.

Summary

- Given the tax advantages, appreciation potential, loan reduction, and eventual increase in rents due to inflation, a "break-even" cash flow will turn out to be a good investment for the long-term investor.

- For the purposes of screening the profitability of potential investments, total operating expenses for most small apartment buildings can be estimated at 45% of gross rents.

- It is important to determine the true market rents of a potential purchase, as these rents may or may not be the same as the current rent roll.

- Profitability in today's market can be razor thin and it is essential to *accurately* predict cash flows by using the correct numbers for total operating expenses and rental income.

VALUING PROPERTY 7

In addition to having a positive cash flow, you must be certain that you do not pay too much for your investment *and* you must ensure that the property is likely to appreciate in value over time. We have shown how to determine cash flows, but how do we determine if the asking price is high, low, or just right? In short, how do we determine the *real* value or *fair market* value of the property we are considering? Fair market value can be defined as follows:

Fair market value is the price that a buyer would be willing to pay and a seller would be willing to accept on the open market assuming a reasonable period of time for an agreement to arise.

The necessary characteristics of a fair market transaction are:

1. buyer and seller are typically motivated;

2. both parties are well informed or well advised, and each acting in what he or she considers his or her own best interest;

3. a reasonable time is allowed for exposure in the open market;

4. payment is made in terms of cash in U.S. dollars or in terms of financial arrangements comparable thereto; and,

5. the price represents the normal consideration for the property sold unaffected by special or creative financing or sales concessions granted by anyone associated with the sale.

If any of these characteristics are untrue, then the possibility exists that you are buying above or below fair market value. Notice that such deviations can benefit *either* the buyer or the seller. For example, a very motivated uninformed seller who has not listed his or her property on the open market presents an ideal opportunity to buy property below market value. On the other hand, if *you* are the emotional (overly) motivated buyer and the seller is informed and you are not, then *you* are likely to pay above market value for your investment. Unfortunately there is no blue print for determining property values. No one can know for sure *how* motivated a typical buyer or seller was or what "a reasonable time on the market" is. Even professional appraisers will agree that valuing property is part art and part science. Fortunately, for us, there are a number of acceptable methods for determining fair market value that we can apply. If we apply these methods, and try and keep our emotions at bay, we will have the necessary data to ascertain whether the sale price is high, low, or just right.

Methods for Valuing Property

There are three common approaches used to appraise the value of rental property. The first method is the comparative sale approach. The second method is income based and utilizes methods such as cap rates and gross rent multipliers (GRMs) to estimate value. The third method is the replacement cost approach. We will cover all three of these methods in the following sections.

The Comparative Sales Approach

The comparative sales approach is by far the most common method used to calculate the market value of rental property, especially for residential single-family homes and small apartments of 2–4 units. For commercial properties (>4 units), this method is less important, and the income approaches should be given more weight. In general, the more units there are in the building, the more credence should be placed on income methods of calculating property value. When using the comparative sale approach, your comparative property, or "comp" should have the following characteristics.

1. **Date of sale.** A comp should be from a recent sale, ideally less than six months and no more than one year. A property that is listed for sale but not sold cannot be a comp.

2. **Proximity.** A comp should be close to the subject property, preferably in the same neighborhood.

3. **Physical attributes.** A comp should have similar physical features such as age, condition, type of construction (slab, crawl, one story, two story, brick), square footage, number of units, number of bedrooms, bathrooms, parking, lot size, amenities (garage, pool, decks), etc.

Obviously, the more recent the sale, and the closer the attributes match your subject property, the better the comparable. When there are significant attribute differences between the subject property and your comp, then this method is harder to apply. One may need to make adjustments for differences in square footage, number of bathrooms, or other features that are different. Appraisers are experts at this and can readily add or subtract from the subject property to account for these differences. Even for professionals, however, this adjustment process can be misleading. For example, let's suppose you find a duplex that sold within six months, which was identical in every respect to the subject property except the comparable sale had two baths per unit whereas the property you are interested in has only one-bath per unit. An appraiser would quickly subtract $5,000 for the additional bathroom and proudly present you with a number. Is this value accurate though? Not if tenants in that area insist upon having two bathrooms and the inventory of two bath units is high. You may find you can't rent the one-bath units for similar rents as the two-bath units. You may find, in fact, this is why the seller is unloading these properties. In such a case, you then need to be prepared to physically add this required second bath in order to own a viable rental property. You may find that walls need to be rearranged and building permits are required, and in fact the actual cost to add on the bath is closer to $15,000. So we see that *property type features* that were discussed earlier play a very large role, often far beyond even what a trained appraiser may estimate. In short, this adjustment method is very dangerous to apply to investment properties. Although most other real estate books encourage adjustments on comparables, I discourage it for the aforementioned reasons. If you can not find any good comparables, you can challenge the seller's agent to prove to you why the property is worth the asking price. Ask for examples of comparables and compare his or her analysis to yours. If there are truly no recent sales to compare to, be aware that you are taking a risk. In these cases I would go back further than one year to look for potential comparables. If you find these older comparables, you can then adjust using the estimated appreciation of your area (the method to predict appreciation rates is presented later). The bottom line is that you need *some* type of comparable before you buy a single-family or small apartment building. If there are none, you are forced to use other methods, such as the income or replacement costing approaches, which are not as accurate on these smaller properties. As a final resort, you can pay an appraiser to independently appraise the real estate you are interested in. If you choose this course, make sure that they have a distinguished track record on appraising investment properties, as this service will cost you a minimum of several hundred dollars.

We haven't yet discussed *how* to obtain comps. If you are working with a real estate agent, this is your best source to find recent (comparable) sales. If not, you can usually find this information on the Internet. You should first look to see if you have a website for your county or city tax records. Most cities provide this online service to the public. Additionally, there are Internet sites where one can access historical property sales. To find these websites, search under "home estimators" or "home value." You will get a lot of links to realtor websites but if you persist, you will find some search engines that access tax records organized by city, county, or zip codes. Essentially you need to research until you can accumulate enough data to suggest that the asking price on the subject property is supported by recent sales.

In summary, for single-family homes and small apartment buildings, the comparative sales approach is an important indicator of value. For larger properties, however, the comparable sales approach may be less useful. For these properties, income approaches such as the cap rate method must be used to predict value.

The Capitalization Rate Approach— "Cap Rates"

To understand capitalization rates (cap rates), let's begin by looking at the equation used to calculate them:

$$\text{Cap Rate} = \frac{\text{NOI}}{\text{Value}} \qquad \text{NOI} = \text{Total income} - \text{Total expenses}$$

As we saw before in our calculation of debt coverage ratios, NOI is simply your total net income minus your total operating expenses (not including your debt). Value, of course, is sale price. So really, cap rate is no different than a dividend on a stock or interest rate on bond. For a $100,000 property that nets $5,000 per year, one obtains a cap rate of 0.05, or a 5% return rate. It is important to recognize that cap rate doesn't factor in your financing. It is the reported return as if you paid cash for your property.

Cap rates are used to predict value on properties by merit of their income-producing capabilities. Rearranging our equation we obtain:

$$\text{Value} = \frac{\text{NOI}}{\text{Cap Rate}}$$

Thus, if one knows the *market cap rate* and NOI, one can estimate property value. The following example illustrates use of cap rates to determine property value. We will use the same duplex example we used in Chapter 6. To begin we first need to calculate NOI. If we use the same assumptions we used in Chapter 6 for vacancy and operating expenses, NOI is determined as follows:

Gross Rental Income	$16,800
Less Vacancy Rate (5%)	–$840
Net Rental Income	**$15,960**
Less Operating Expenses (45% gross rents)	–$7,560
Net Operating Income (NOI)	**$8,400**

If we determine that the market cap rates in this area are 5%–6%, knowing the NOI we can estimate property value:

Property value estimate based upon a cap rate of 5%:

$$\text{Value} = \frac{\text{NOI}}{\text{Cap Rate}} = \frac{\$8,400}{0.05} = \$168,000$$

Property value estimate based upon a cap rate of 6%:

$$\text{Value} = \frac{\text{NOI}}{\text{Cap Rate}} = \frac{\$8,400}{0.06} = \$140,000$$

As you can see, very small differences in cap rates can lead to a very large difference in price. Thus, in order to effectively use cap rates to predict value, you must be able to *accurately* determine the *market cap rates* for the subject property at hand. Accurately predicting market cap rates for a given property and area is challenging, and one reason why using cap rates can be tedious to use and are best reserved for larger apartment buildings. Cap rates are useful, however, when taken together with the other methods of valuation and we can not ignore them.

A good method to find out the market cap rate for a given property and area is to contact a local bank that deals in real estate investment loans. Banks need to keep track of cap rates because they use them in evaluating loans for investors. The debt coverage (DCR) method can prove to the bank whether the property will cover the debt, but cap rates can provide an indication of property value as well as potential risk of the investment. If the cap rate on a property is out of line with the market cap rate, there may be a risk involved for the bank. When I call, I usually ask for the construction loan department. Find a knowledgeable lender and ask them what the cap rates are for residential income properties. Tell them you are thinking of taking out a construction loan and want to know the criteria they use for appraising new construction values on income properties using cap rates. Ask them how they calculate their NOI (you may need to use their NOI assumptions if they are different from those presented here). In addition to banks, another good method for obtaining market cap rates is to contact seller's agents or appraisers in your area that deal exclusively with investment real estate. Using these resources, you should have a good idea of what the market cap rates would be for a given area and property. Once again, ask how they calculate their NOI to understand what their assumptions are regarding expenses and vacancy rates

Stated Cap Rates

When looking for real estate and reviewing information provided by the seller's agent, be aware of *stated cap rates*. *Stated cap rates* are not actual cap rates. Many sellers or realtors improperly calculate the cap rate, leaving out operating costs or overestimating income, all of which can give the perception of a higher cap rate than is actually the case. If you use the guidelines provided here and in Chapter 6 for predicting income and expenses, however, you should be able to come up with an accurate NOI and thus an accurate cap rate.

Understanding Cap Rates

If you consider the cap rate equation like a mathematician, high cap rates and high profitability can result from high NOI (rents) and/or low property values. Low cap rates and low profitability can result from low NOI and/or high property values:

$$\text{Cap Rate} = \frac{\text{NOI}}{\text{Value}} \quad \begin{array}{l} \text{If NOI} \uparrow \text{ and/or Value} \downarrow \text{ then Cap Rate} \uparrow \\ \text{If NOI} \downarrow \text{ and/or Value} \uparrow \text{ then Cap Rate} \downarrow \end{array}$$

In the last few years cap rate trends have followed interest rates and thus both have declined to the lowest levels seen since the mid 1960s. This decrease in cap rates has been due to property values *increasing* while rents (NOI) remain *stable to falling*. This upward pressure on property values from the availability of lower interest rates also coincides with a period of low stock market returns and the feeling that "you can't go wrong" in real estate. In fact, rents, and thus NOI, have declined in many cities across the country as renters continue to leave the rental market and buy their first homes. More renters today than ever before qualify for owner-occupied housing due to low mortgage rates. A recent discussion with a loan investor in our city indicated renters are being offered zero percent down loans on condominiums where the total (interest-only) mortgage payment is $550 per month. This combination of low rents (NOI ↓) and high property values (Value ↑) has led to these historically low cap rates.

If cap rates tend to follow interest rates, a logical question is what effect a sharp increase in interest rates would have on cap rates. A recent study from Moody's Investment Service addressed this question and more.[10] The study found that composite cap rates from 1965–2003 were 9.8%, whereas current cap rates[11] were around 8.8%, or at historic lows. The variance by region, demographic, and socioeconomic conditions was large. In certain regions in California for example, investors were purchasing apartment buildings with 5–6% cap rates. The study goes on to state that this trend toward lower interest rates and thus lower capitalization rates and higher property value appreciation is likely not sustainable in the long-term.

With cap rates and interest rates at historical lows, one may ask if we should be investing in real estate at all. Is investing in real estate now like jumping in the stock market when it is overvalued and trading at historically high price to earnings (PE) ratios? Similar to the stock market, no one has a crystal ball and the decision to invest, therefore, needs to be yours. You do need to be aware of the risks, however. The biggest risk with investing in a low cap rate environment is that there is an interest rate risk associated with such purchases. If cap rates and interest rates are at historical lows, and interest rates rise, properties lose value. Why? If interest rates rise then cap rates will also rise. If cap rates rise and NOI (rents) remain unchanged or decline, then property value *must* decrease, as can be seen by reviewing the following equation.

$$\text{Value} = \frac{\text{NOI}}{\text{Cap Rate}} \qquad \text{If NOI} \leftrightarrow \text{and Cap Rate} \uparrow \text{then Value} \downarrow$$

In addition to cap rates following interest rate trends, another cap rate truism is that historical cap rate values have remained higher than prevailing interest rates. Why is this so? If interest rates were to rise *above* the cap rate of your property you would have trouble selling the property because it now returns *less* than the prevailing interest rate. This means your property has less value now. After all, since cap rate returns are really just a measure of return on investment, why would one go though the bother of owning real estate for the same return they can get on a ten-year Treasury bill? This interest rate effect on real estate value is somewhat analogous to buying a bond at a 8% return and while you own it interest rates increase to 10%. The value of your bond goes down because no one is willing to buy your bond at face value when they can buy a new bond that pays a 10% return.

There is in fact, a *rule of thumb* that investors use that relates current interest rates to cap rates. All things being equal, a *good* cap rate, and thus a profitable property, needs to be 1–2% higher than the prevailing mortgage interest rates.[12]

To conclude then, investments with historically low cap rates (low returns) are more sensitive to interest/financing costs as higher financing costs can turn an otherwise good investment into a poor one. This is one of the problems with adjustable rate mortgages (ARMs) on investment property. A property with an 8% cap rate may look great with a 4% ARM (4% below cap rate) but may cost you money (negative cash flow) if the interest rate rises to 7% (1% below cap rate). Many investors consider the financing package only in current terms and they forget that they may need to refinance in three, five, or seven years. What will the income of the property be then, and what will the interest rates be? It's always better to start with a higher cap rate whenever possible, as the answers to future income and interest rate questions are unknown.

Cap Rates and Short-Term Financing

There is an additional risk for investors using short-term financing. If property values suddenly drop due to rising interest rates, lenders may require more cash when refinancing to cover the loss in value. For commercial loans, lenders require you to maintain a 75–80% LTV. If you had $250,000 down on a $1,000,000 apartment building ($750,000; 75% LTV), and that property is now valued at $800,000 instead of $1,000,000, due to an increase in interest rates and cap rates, the bank is concerned because your LTV has now increased from 75% to 94% ($750,000 ÷ $ 800,000). For an $800,000 property value, at 75% LTV, the bank will only lend you $600,000. Since the bank is currently loaning you $750,000, the bank may demand the difference ($150,000) from you to bring your loan within the 75% LTV. Such a change in interest rates could thus have a devastating effect on investments, especially when made with a low cap rate purchase (5–6%), as is currently becoming more common.

The bottom line is that by using fixed-term financing you avoid one of the major risks of buying properties with low cap rates—namely, no one can force you to come up with cash, refinance, or sell. Unfortunately you do not usually have this option when purchasing larger apartment buildings or other commercial real estate. With these types of investments, therefore, one must pay close attention to cap rates, interest rates, and their current trends in order to make informed decisions.

Future Trends

If current cap rates may be too low, what about future trends in cap rates? The summary opinion from Moody's Special Report 31 regarding the future trends of cap rates was stated as follows:

- Low cap rates have been pushing up property values and this increase has coincided with a decrease in fundamentals, such as NOI.

- Both cap rates and commercial mortgage rates are at historically low levels.

- Cap rates are likely to rise from current levels within the term of most loans, although we do not expect rates to return to the high (cap rate) levels of the early 1990s.

- Capital could shift away from real estate just as it flowed into the (real estate) asset markets, which would result in a decrease in value and increase in cap rates.

The upshot of the report was as follows. The low interest rate environment, and more importantly, the *spread* between interest rates and cap rates, has been the driver in increasing property values across the United States. In short, lower interest rates have *pulled* down cap rates in order to maintain their historical spread. At the same time, NOI cash flows from rents (inflation) has been stagnant, thus the overall effect of lowering cap rates (NOI↔, Value ↑, Cap Rate ↓). The other obvious factor contributing to the increase in real estate values is the dismal contribution of stocks in recent history, leading to a "historical record influx of cash into the mortgage equity markets." The risk of a rise in mortgage rates in such a low cap rate environment could be devastating to investors. A table was presented as a very compelling reason to be fearful of such interest rate increases if you are investing using commercial (short-term) financing.

Effect of Interest Rate Increases on Debt Coverage Ratios (DCR)*

Loan Terms

NOI	Loan	Cap Rate	Value (NOI/Cap Rate)	LTV
$100,000	$937,000	8%	$1,250,000	75%

Impact of Rising Mortgage Rates on DCR

Interest Rate	6%	8%	10%	12%
DCR	1.47	1.20	1.01	0.86

*Taken from Moody's Special Report March, 2003

So we see that at a constant cap rate of 8% ($100,000 NOI ÷ $1,250,000 value) and a 75% LTV loan, if interest rates move from 8% to 10%, then DCR moves from 1.20 (profitable) to 1.01 (barely breaking even). Clearly then, any dramatic increase in mortgage rates could materially affect cash flow and thus the refinance risk of mortgage bonds. The corollary of this viewpoint is that interest rates may remain at low (near) historical levels while the economy strengthens. In such an environment, property values would increase as NOI increases due to inflationary upward pressure on rents (NOI ↑, Cap Rate ↔, Value ↑).

Regardless of what the future holds, these are clearly sobering facts for those who are considering financing their investment with any type of (commercial) balloon payment that would require a refinance in the next several years. Smaller properties, single-family, duplexes, triplexes, and quadraplexes should remain largely exempt from this type of risk, as they can be purchased with long-term fixed conventional Fannie Mae or Freddie Mac financing. Property values for these dwellings may drop as well if interest rates increase, but at least you won't be vulnerable to negative cash flows, or worst yet, having to come up with large sums of cash to meet the required loan to value. Since your loan is fixed for the long term, you can "ride out" these down turns in property values while your DCR (and cash flow) remains fixed to the length of your loan.

In summary, cap rates can be used as a predictor of property value if your estimates of NOI and *market cap rates* are accurate. In contrast to the comparable sales method, which is used primarily for single-family and small multifamily apartment buildings (1–4 units), cap rate valuations are primarily used for larger unit buildings (>4 units). If you are looking at one of these larger properties, be sure you obtain accurate market cap rates for your area so you can estimate property value accurately. Also, remember that there is a relationship between interest rates and cap rates. If interest rates rise, there is an upward pressure on cap rates to rise as well. If cap rates increase without a rise in rents (NOI), property values must decrease. For these reasons, investing in commercial properties carries a higher risk than investing in properties that can be financed with conventional long-term financing. If interest rates increase and you have short-term commercial grade financing, you will need to refinance at a higher interest rate. At a higher interest rate, your yearly debt will increase, which will result in lower profitability along with the lower property values.

Using GRMs to Predict Value

As we learned in Chapter 5, the gross rent multiplier (GRM) is a useful tool for pinpointing profitable areas to invest in. The equation we used was the following.

$$ GRM \ = \ \frac{Price}{Rent} $$

If we rearrange the GRM equation and substitute value for price we obtain:

$$ Value = Rent \times GRM $$

For our purposes, rent is defined as monthly gross rents, and GRM is a predetermined factor. The GRM method of estimating market value is the most popular, probably because it is easiest to understand. We know, however, that the "easy way" is often not the "best way." In fact, GRMs are at best crude estimates of value, as they are based upon gross rents and thus don't even factor in such things such as vacancy rates or operating expenses. The GRM method, therefore, should be weighted the least when valuing income properties.

Like cap rate returns and cash flows, GRMs are specific to area and investment risk. High GRM areas usually have a higher risk and lower likelihood of appreciation. Low GRMs are typically found in more established neighborhoods where risk is low but historical appreciation has been high. We used this attribute of GRMs in Chapter 5 to identify high-, medium-, and low-risk investment areas. In order to use GRMs to predict value, you must determine the market GRM for the area of the subject property. Chapter 5 goes into more detail on how to generate GRMs for your subject properties. Similar to market cap rates, the more confidence you have in your market GRM factor, the more accurate this approach will be when calculating property values. The inexact nature of GRMs as a tool for predicting value can be best illustrated by example. For a duplex with $700 per side per month income ($1,400 per month) in an area with market GRMs of 110–130, the following value would be estimated:

$$Value = Rent \times GRM$$

For a GRM of 110:
$$Value = \$1,400 \times 110 = \$154,000$$

For a GRM of 130:
$$Value = \$1,400 \times 130 = \$182,000$$

NOTE:
You should have already done a GRM screening exercise as part of selecting your target area as described in Chapter 5. If you have, then you already know the market GRM and can easily use this GRM range to predict value.

As you can see, this is why GRMs can fall short when used as a tool to calculate value. GRM spreads are often large due to location differences (micro and macro), age, property attributes, rents, etc. One should also note that a small difference in rent per month could greatly impact your predicted value.

In summary then, although the GRM method for predicting value is less precise than other income methods, it is a popular method due to its ease of understanding. This method should be used in conjunction with more exact methods such as the cap rate method.

Replacement Cost Approach

The theory of the replacement cost approach (also known as the reproduction method) is that the value of a property can be estimated by summing the land value and the depreciated value of any improvements. The assumption is that if you combine the worth of the land with the cost to replace the building sitting on the land, and then adjust for the age of your subject property, you have the market value of your subject property.

The problem with this technique is that it is not very accurate in more established areas where vacant lots are no longer available. In other words, it is hard to calculate the worth of the land alone when there is none for sale. Nevertheless, this method should be used in your value determinations, as it provides a "reality check," so to speak. If the value you get using this approach is very divergent from those obtained from cap rates, GRMs, or comparable sales, it may be cause for concern. To illustrate the use of the reproduction method, let's look at an example using our familiar duplex. Since there are no vacant lots in this area, we adjust for available similar lots nearby and come up with a value for the land of $50,000. The subject property is 2,300 square feet. Building costs in our area for this type of construction are approximately $100 per square foot. This means the building would cost $230,000 to build new. Since the building in our example is twenty years old, we assume that half of its useful life is therefore used up. The (depreciated) replacement worth of the building is therefore $115,000. Combining the value of the land and depreciated cost of the building, we obtain $165,000, which in this case, is close to what we were obtaining using other methods. This method, however, is flawed on several levels. Deciding the useful life of a building is arbitrary. The forty years used as the typical useful economic life is a number derived from the IRS and corresponds to the depreciation life of residential real estate. The useful economic life for tax purposes, however, is not the same as the actual physical life expectancy of residential property. Most structures are quite robust after forty years and they would be worth more than zero dollars. This method also assumes that the building and the materials only depreciate over time and do not appreciate in value. This is again not true as lumber costs today are probably twice what they were twenty years ago. Much like the GRM method of predicting value, the replacement approach should be used only in conjunction with the comparable sales approach and cap rate method. It shouldn't be weighted heavily, but it is a good way to ensure that property prices are not artificially inflated. If the value determined by the cost replacement approach is very different from values obtained using the other methods, you should try and understand why. It may be a signal that a real estate bubble is in effect.

Putting it All Together

In summary, we have presented three approaches to determining the value of real estate: the comparable sales (comp) method, the cap rate and GRM income methods, and the replacement cost method. In order to understand the value of your prospective purchase, you are encouraged to perform all of these costing methods but weigh them differently for each property type. For single-family homes in predominantly owner-occupied neighborhoods, the comparative approach should be used exclusively. When estimating property values for 2–4 units, the comparative sales approach should be used as the primary indicator, with cap rate, GRM, and replacement methods used as supporting information. For buildings of larger than four units, commercial banking rules apply, and the comparative sales approach should not be weighted heavily. In these cases, the cap rate and GRM income methods and replacement cost approach should be used to appraise property values.

> TIP: During the negotiation phase I usually exploit the valuation methods that predict lower value to try and bring the seller down in price.

The Final Check—Is the Property Likely to Appreciate?

Determining the value of your real estate purchase is important to ensure you don't pay too much for your property. As a final check, though, you need to ensure that your property is likely to appreciate over time, rather than depreciate. Like stocks and other investments, we can only use historical trends as our guide. In short, you will need to find out what the same type of properties sold for as far back in time as you can go. Find out what the owners paid when they bought their properties and tabulate the sales data over the years. This tax record data should be available on the Internet. If you cannot get this information from the Internet and don't wish to spend the time at the county court house or local library, help from a realtor or appraiser may be necessary. By performing this analysis, you can determine if the trend is upward or downward. Normally you will find an upward trend over a five- or ten-year period. If you find the trend is flat or edging downward, do not buy in the subject property area.

Real Estate Bubbles

It is undeniable that any investment vehicle is subject to cycles. These swings can be due to fundamental drivers, such as supply and demand, as well as speculative forces. When speculative forces dominate, prices can be driven to unsustainable or *bubble levels*. Real estate is no exception to this rule. Although we may have the tools to determine property values in similar geographic and demographic areas, such market valuation ignores the bigger question of whether the market itself is overvalued. This is especially disturbing at this point in history, when housing prices are currently at historical highs. This increase in housing prices is actually a worldwide phenomenon, where in fact the United States is actually somewhat behind other nations such as Britain and Australia. The recent worldwide boom in house prices has been driven principally by two common factors: the availability of cheap financing, and the fact that investors have lost faith in the stock market after the year 2000 stock market crash. *Interest-only* and *no-money-down mortgages*, coupled with low-interest rate ARMs, have allowed buyers to borrow more money and afford to buy investment homes or upgrade to more expensive owner-occupied homes. The statistics are startling. A study by the NAR found that in 2004, fully 23% of all American houses were bought for investment purposes and not owner occupation. In the same year, an additional 12% of the homes purchased were vacation homes. Thus, a surprising 35% of all homes purchased in this year were for investment purposes! In many cases, investors were willing to buy houses that would rent at a loss in the hopes that appreciation would make up for negative cash flows.

How do we know if the current property values are sustainable, or whether prices have been boosted by speculation to bubble levels? Since the existence of a bubble can only be proven after it breaks, the answer is that we can't answer this question yet. There is, however, a great deal of research on the topic and experts appear to be well divided. The most compelling argument that U.S. home prices are currently overvalued is that the ratio of home prices to rent is 35% above its average level seen during the period of 1975–2000. To bring the home price to rent ratio back to normal, either rents must rise or prices must fall. Given the current low rate of inflation, the former is unlikely. If rents were to rise 2.5% per year, house prices would need to remain flat for twelve years to bring the U.S. ratio of house prices to rent back to its long-term norm. It has been proposed that the recent housing boom is due to the availability of low-interest financing, but can interest rates alone account for this current real estate pricing? Calculations suggest that a single percentage point change in conventional loan interest rates would theoretically affect home prices by about 10%. For interest-only mortgages, this same calculation yields about a 16% change for a 1% change in interest rates at current rates. A 2% drop in long-term interest rates could then account for about a 20% (10% X 2%) rise in home prices if every buyer is using a fixed-rate mortgage. ARMs have dropped three points during this period, so if everyone had used an ARM, the projected price increase would be about 50% (16 X 3% = 48%). The actual increase in valuations for the United States during this period has been about 45% and is thus consistent with this predicted increase. The lower interest rates may rationalize some of the price increases, but many metropolitan area prices rose well above 50% during this period.

Although we now are in a bubble, when one considers holding periods in excess of a decade the picture looks different. Yale economist and *Irrational Exuberance* author Robert J. Shiller demonstrated that even when one includes our current "bubble" levels, inflation-adjusted U.S. home prices increased only 0.4% per year from 1890 to 2004. Shiller has showed comparable results for housing prices on a single street in Amsterdam (the site of the fabled tulip mania, and where the housing supply is notably limited) going back over a 350-year period! Although the averages clearly favor the long-term investor, local housing corrections are real and can take very long to recover, as the following figure illustrates. This data on historical price declines and recovery periods was taken over a twenty-five-year period from selected U.S. cites.

	Peak to Trough Decline	Duration	Time required to climb back to original peak
Boston	25%	5 years	9 years
New York	10.0%	7 years	11 years
Los Angeles	21.4%	7 years	9 years
San Francisco	3.8%	4 years	7 years
Houston	23.1%	5 years	9 years
Honolulu	24%	9 years	13 years

Source: National Association of Realtors

In these historical examples, if your timing was bad, you would need to wait, in some cases, a full decade or longer before you would recover your capital losses. Regardless of whether there is a national housing bubble, clearly there are geographic areas where the recent price increases don't make sense in historical terms and may not be sustainable in the short-term. When investing in these areas, you should ensure your cash flows cover expenses and that the financing is long-term and fixed. If you maintain this investing strategy and are prepared to hold for the long term, you should be able to weather down turns until prices return.

Summary

- The three common approaches used to appraise the value of real estate is the comparative sales method, the income methods (cap rate and GRM), and the replacement cost method.

- For single-family homes in predominantly owner-occupied neighborhoods, the comparative sales approach should be used exclusively to determine value.

- When estimating property values for two to four units, the comparative sales approach should be used along with the income and replacement methods.

- For buildings of larger than four units, commercial banking rules apply, and the cap rate income method should be used to appraise property values.

- All things being equal, a *good* cap rate, and thus a profitable property, needs to be 1–2% higher than the prevailing mortgage interest rate.

- Investing in commercial properties (more than four units) carries an interest rate risk because conventional long-term fixed financing is often not possible.

- Determining the market value of a property does not take into consideration larger economic factors, such as the existence of real estate bubbles.

- The existence of a bubble can only be proven after it breaks.

FINANCING YOUR INVESTMENT

8

How you finance your investment is extremely important. The type of loan you choose dictates your cash flow and thus affects your profitability. Because of this, you should shop for financing before you buy or even begin looking. In broad terms, there are two types of financing available: *conventional loans* and *commercial loans*. *Conventional loans* are the loans familiar to most homeowners, where the interest rate can be fixed for the term of the loan, typically fifteen or thirty years. This type of financing is available for single-family homes, duplexes, triplexes, and quadraplexes (one to four units). These loans are backed by and conform to the quasi-government organizations of Fannie Mae and Freddie Mac. Conventional loans are available for both owner-occupied purchases as well as non-owner (investment) purchases. If the purchase is for investment purposes, then typically a slightly higher interest rate is charged than if the property is intended for owner occupancy.

Investment property having more than five units typically cannot be financed with a conventional loan and must be financed with a commercial loan. *Commercial loans* can also be fixed for extended periods, but unlike a conventional loan, commercial loans typically have a balloon payment where the loan becomes due before the term is up. The focus of the following discussions will largely be on conventional financing options for one to four units, as they pose the least risk to the investor of small apartment buildings. The latter section will be devoted to the commercial financing of properties with more than five units.

Fixed-Rate, Adjustable-Rate, and Interest-Only Loans

Deciding whether to go with a fixed-rate loan, short- or long-term, or an adjustable rate mortgage (ARM) fixed for one, three, five, seven, or ten years, or a so-called *interest-only loan,* can be an overwhelming decision. Obviously, the shorter the term of the loan in fixed-rate financing, the higher the principal portion of the payment will be, and thus the higher your monthly payment will be. ARMs have lower interest rates, which result in lower principal and interest (PI) payments but are not fixed for the entire term. Because ARMs are not fixed for the entire term of the loan, there is interest rate risk beyond the initial (fixed) term. Interest-only loans have no principal component so your loan amount never gets reduced over time. They do, however, offer a very low payment, as the principal part of PI is "absent." In deciding which option you choose, I would stay away from ARMs with fixed rates of less than five years unless you plan on selling within this time frame. In keeping with at least a five-year fixed rate, you minimize the risk that interest rates could increase before you have some appreciation in your property. The second important point is to ensure your property has a positive cash flow for the type of loan you choose. If your investment breaks even with a ten-year fixed loan, then go for it. It makes no sense, however, to choose a ten-year fixed loan if your cash flow will be negative unless you are willing to make up the difference every month. If you are average in your luck, however, a thirty-year loan will be necessary to achieve a break-even or better cash flow with 20% down payment.

In summary then, the loan you select should be chosen based upon your cash flow predictions. You should strive to minimize the term length of the loan (maximize the principal portion) without going into a negative cash flow mode.

Regardless of the type of loan you choose, you will undoubtedly ask yourself, "Should I pay off my loan early by making extra principal payments?" To answer this question, let's consider each of the extremes in turn, the first case where you pay off your loan quickly, and the second where you maintain a higher debt. In the case where you are making accelerated payments or have a shorter loan term, such as a ten-year fixed rate, you will eventually reach your goal and have the loan paid off. At this point, you have 100% of your money invested in that single property. On a $170,000 purchase, if property values go up 5%, your return on investment (ROI) is 5% of $170,000, or $8,500. I think most financial planners would agree that 5% is not a good return. In fact, you could do better investing in stocks or bonds, or as we shall see, investing in more real estate. Now consider the opposite extreme, where you get a thirty-year loan and make no additional principal payments. From our previous example, if you put down 20% on $170,000, or $34,000, and property values go up 5%, your return is $8,500 on your down payment of $34,000. This is actually a 25% return. This is the power of *leveraging*, which was discussed in Chapter 1. The ability to leverage is what makes investing in real estate such a wealth-building enterprise. In fact, without it, you *would* be better off investing in stocks and bonds. The bottom line is, as you can see when comparing the two scenarios, that as you continue to pay down your fixed-term loan, you are earning a progressively lower and lower return on your investment.

One may argue, however, that it is better to pay down your loan, at least in the early years, because fixed rate mortgages are *front-loaded* with interest. That is to say, you pay more interest in the early years of your loan. This is in fact not true. I will show that you *never* pay more than your fixed interest rate at any point in the amortization schedule. In fact, there is no intrinsic financial argument for paying off your loan any faster than the bank or mortgage company dictates. This is especially true in a low-interest rate environment. Rather than pay down $20,000 on a loan, I would *leverage* my money by buying another positive cash flow property. In this way, you ensure a *maximum rate of return* and will therefore achieve financial independence at a faster rate. In order to appreciate this argument more fully, one needs to comprehend how amortization schedules work.

Understanding Amortization

In order to appreciate amortization, one must decipher the cryptic tables of amortization schedules. Amortization schedules appear complicated, but they are actually quite simple. To understand amortization, let's look at a typical amortization schedule and try to understand where the numbers come from. For our example, the loan amount is $136,000 (20% down on $170,000). The interest rate is 6% and the loan has a 30-year fixed term. The monthly PI payment on this loan is $815.39. The amortization schedule for this loan is shown in the figure below. For clarity, we have deleted all the intervening years and left only the 1-, 5-, 10-, 15-, and 30-year payments.

Payment = $815.39	Principal	Interest	Balance
Payment 1 (start loan)	$135.39	$680.00	$135,864.61
Payment 12 (1 year)	$143.03	$672.36	$134,329.89
Payment 60 (5 years)	$181.71	$633.68	$126,553.84
Payment 120 (10 years)	$245.10	$570.29	$113,812.38
Payment 180 (15 years)	$330.61	$484.78	$96,626.05
Payment 360 (30 years)	$815.39	$0.00	$0.00

As you can see, in progressing down the table, the principal portion of the payment increases when compared to the interest portion, until finally in the last payment (Payment 360) the entire payment goes toward principal and the loan is paid off. To start (Payment 1), your principal is $135.39 and your interest is $680.00. With your first payment you are thus paying $680 interest on the $136,000 you borrowed, which is $680 / $136,000, or 0.5% per month, which is 6% per year. The balance after your first payment is thus $136,000 less $135.39 (principal) or $135,864.61. After 10 years (Payment 120) you owe a balance of $113,812.38 and you are paying $570.29 interest on this amount, which is still 6% per year ($570.29 ÷ $113,812 x 12 = 6%). So you see, the interest is not "front-loaded" or "higher" in the early years of your mortgage as we often hear. The interest you pay in a fixed-rate loan is always the exact amount you locked your rate in at, in this case 6%. The difference, of course, is that the proportion of principal becomes larger, and interest smaller, the further you go down the amortization table. The effect of pre-paying your loan or making "extra" principal payments is to "jump" down the amortization table. In the extreme case, let's consider the effect of making an extra principal payment of $22,187.62 for your first payment. You would then owe $113,812.38 ($136,000 – $22,187.62) and would "jump" to Payment 120 (10 years) on the amortization schedule. Your monthly principal component would then be, from this point on, higher ($245.10 for this payment). You still, however, pay your 6% rate on the loan balance. That never changes for the entire term.

So what then is the correct answer? Should you make extra (principal) payments to accelerate the reduction of your loans? Should you choose longer or shorter term mortgages? I can only help with half of the answer here. The reason is that there are always two correct answers in the world of personal financial planning. One is a financial (calcu-lated) answer; the other is an emotional answer. The correct financial answer is that it makes more sense to opt for the lower payment amount, longer loan terms, and then to reinvest the extra monthly cash flow either into real estate (a new purchase) or the stock market. In this way, you maximize your percent return on dollars invested and you don't end up with hundreds of thousands of dollars earning (poor) real estate returns of 2–5% per year.[13]

Taken to the extreme then, one could argue that "interest-only" loans make the most sense. Without having to contribute a principal portion, you are maximizing your leveraging ability by using these loans. What I don't like about interest-only loans is that you miss out on one of the most beneficial aspects of owning rental property, namely having someone else pay down your mortgage over time. Another argument in favor of carrying more debt, as opposed to paying off your mortgage on an accelerated schedule, is the added tax advantages of writing off the interest every year.

> NOTE:
> When buying property in areas that have high cash flows but lower appreciation potential, consider shorter mortgage terms such as ten or fifteen years. These shorter-term mortgages accelerate your equity buildup by mortgage pay down. Conversely, in areas where appreciation potential is greater and cash flows are low, you will likely need to go for the longer-term, lower-payment mortgages, to meet cash flow needs.

If this was the correct financial answer to whether you should accelerate your loan payments, what is the emotional answer? If you are debt adverse and it is your goal in life to burn that mortgage paper in ten years and collect the full rent checks every month, then by all means go ahead and pay down that loan as quickly as you can. In such cases, if you can afford it, your emotions should dictate your decision. Since I believe the truth always lies somewhere in the middle, my guidelines for selecting financing for long-term investing are as follows.

The Five Rules of Financing Your Properties

1. Pay no less than 20% down on any real estate purchase. If you pay less than 20%, you typically have to pay private mortgage insurance, which adds nothing to your bottom line.

2. Choose fixed loans of ten- to thirty-year amortization schedules chosen to ensure a positive cash flow. In this way you ensure that your tenants will be paying down your loan, not you.

3. If you decide to choose an ARM, ensure your rate is fixed for at least five years. A period of five years allows enough time to assure that you have paid off a good chunk of your mortgage by the time the loan's lock-in period expires. Only go with an ARM if it significantly lowers your payment; otherwise, it is not worth the additional risk.

4. Invest any extra cash flow toward maintaining and improving properties, then finally into investing in more real estate, and not into paying down existing debts.

5. Interest-only loans only make sense if you plan on selling the property in less than, say, five years. Although they afford lower payments, they are normally offered at higher interest rates than conventional loans.

Please don't misunderstand my position here. I am a great advocate of someday owning rental properties that are completely paid off. I am also in favor of getting this accomplished as rapidly as possible. I am not, however, in favor of coming up with extra cash out of *my* pocket every month to meet this goal. Let the property itself (tenants) pay off your loans. It makes more financial sense to take those extra dollars and invest them in more real estate or stocks and bonds.

As a final note, there are times when it may make sense to accelerate a loan pay off. For example, if the interest rate on your loan is very high, say, greater than 8%. In these cases one could argue that investing any extra money you have in stocks and bonds may not yield a greater return than removing that debt. In our current environment of low interest rates, however, this situation is becoming increasingly less frequent.

The Low Down On No-Down Deals

Creative financing techniques and "no-money-down" schemes have been the topic of many books and late night infomercials. Due to their popularity, these investment methods must be successful at some level. This is evidenced by the many testimonials seen on television and elsewhere. The attraction of these investing strategies is obvious. If you could invest in real estate with no money down and *still* obtain a positive cash flow, why wouldn't you do it? By putting no money down you are actually taking full advantage of leveraging your investment. Additionally, with no money down you can go on to buy an infinite number of properties, as they cost you nothing. What's wrong with this approach, then? For one, I would argue that in our current environment of high housing values and low rents, finding a property that will provide a break-even or positive cash flow with no money down financing is challenging at best. Providing, however, you actually find such a property, there are a great many problems with these schemes. The financing is very complicated for both the buyer and seller. It requires a certain brain type to understand these deals and, more importantly, to convey them in a lucid manner to the seller. Certainly, in a hot real estate market, I do not see why a seller would bother with such a complex deal when another buyer is waiting in the wings with an easy-to-understand offer. These schemes, therefore, require a willing (desperate?) seller, and especially a seller who actually understands what you are proposing. In reality, such opportunities are hard to find. For this reason nearly all these courses or books propose some sort of probability rule, like the 100–10–1 rule, where the investor needs to screen 100 properties and make 10 offers to finally win one deal. One may also argue that such a selection process is risky, as you may screen out the good properties and be left only with the problem properties that no one else wants to buy. For this reason, one needs to be extremely cautious when applying these investing methods, especially if you are just starting out. The other problem with the no-money-down schemes is that they require several sources of financing for a single deal. Typically you can obtain a conventional financing for 80% of the loan to value. The remaining 20%, however, is the financing you need to creatively find a source for. The source for this financing will typically *not* be a fixed-term loan. Because this part of the financing is not fixed, you are adding an additional interest rate risk to the deal. If interest rates escalate after you buy, your payments on the 20% financing will increase. If you didn't allow for this increase in your cash flow calculations, you may find you now have a negative cash flow. This interest rate risk on your non-fixed loans becomes especially dangerous if you own several such no-money-down properties. In such cases, your cash flow losses are compounded and could easily put you out of business. In summary, if you can make a no-money-down scheme work and still have a positive cash flow, and you are willing to take on the additional risks, then go for it. For most investors, however, conventional approaches to investing in real estate will still be the norm.

Cash-Out Refinancing

There is, however, a method whereby you can bypass all of the risks associated with the typical no-money-down strategies and end up owning properties with anywhere from 10% down to actually getting money back from the closing table. The method I refer to is called *cash-out refinancing*. It is easy to understand and, most importantly, it is invisible to the seller. It is also an effective technique in *both* buyer and seller markets. The downside, as we will learn, is that it usually takes a *minimum* of six months to implement. It also requires you to provide (at least) the initial down payment to get started. I will illustrate the method using an actual example.

The only prerequisite here is that the property you propose to buy must have a good cash flow, at least $100 per month after applying the cash flow calculations presented earlier. It also helps if you buy the property somewhat under market value. The following example illustrates how this approach can be applied. In this case, we bought a duplex in a student area for $110,000, which had deferred maintenance (cosmetic only). We were short of cash so we only put 10% down. Because the down payment was less than 20%, we paid private mortgage insurance (PMI), and in this case PMI was an additional $75 per month. We got the seller to pay $2,500 in closing costs, the maximum allowed. He agreed to this because we increased the sale price on the contract from $110,000 to $112,500 to cover the closing costs. In doing this, he ended up with the same cash at closing but we saved $2,500 out of pocket in closing costs. Some astute sellers may point out they have to pay more taxes in capital gains. If that is a problem to them, offer to write a check to cover the additional capital gains. Or, you can just renegotiate the sale price to cover this. It is a small concession and all sellers I have dealt with eventually agree to this. An added tip (don't mention this when you make your offer)—wait until you have a signed contract, then about two weeks later submit this proposal and a revised offer. You don't want to risk the deal by adding a level of complexity at the start. Our loan in this case was 10% of $112,500, or $101,250. Our out-of-pocket at the closing table was $9,000, which is less than 10% (due to the rolling of the $2,500 closing costs into the loan). We then did landscaping, cleaned the house, installed new miniblinds, performed cosmetic improvements, and got both units fully rented. We then carried this loan, with the PMI, for about one year. At this point we contacted our mortgage broker and told her we wanted to do a *cash-out refinance*. We told her we needed an appraised value of at least $150,000, and we helped the mortgage company by providing some recent comparables that sold in the neighborhood, as well as describing *all* the improvements that we had made on the property. We also instructed her that if the property did not appraise for at least $150,000, we would not be interested in refinancing. It is only a slight risk. If the property doesn't appraise, you lose the money you paid for the appraisal and credit report. In such case, you can always just try a different company. So the appraisal came in at $155,000. Our new loan was therefore $124,000 (80% of $155,000). We paid off the old loan of $101,500 and walked away with about $22,500. So after accounting for the original $9,000, we had an additional $13,500, which we used to purchase our next property. This method is somewhat risky because interest rates could increase while you wait for the original loan to season the required six months before a new appraisal is legal. The downside is low, however, as you already have conventional financing in place. If interest rates shoot up you can just petition the mortgage company to drop the PMI based upon your improvements over the years. They usually are receptive to this after a two-year period. If you don't have the cash for the initial down payment, you can take out a home equity line-of-credit on your own home to make the initial down payment. This technique *does* require that you still have a positive cash flow, even after increasing your loan amount and payment. It therefore requires that you factor in the cost of this in your initial cash flow calculations before purchasing.

> **NOTE:**
> Before you attempt a cash-out refinance, be sure to inform yourself on your local lending practices. If you try for a cash-out refinance too soon, the appraiser may need to use your sale as the most recent sale value. This obviously will not help you, as you require a higher appraised value than you paid for the property in order to get cash out.

This method is especially useful after you own property for several years and have built up significant equity. You can perform cash-out refinances and use these dollars to make new purchases. In this way, you can leverage your dollars effectively without paying capital gains as no sale has transpired. Be careful though. I do not recommend going much below 10% equity (90% LTV) on any property in case real estate prices fall. In that case, mortgage companies could require a new loan or cash from you (or PMI) to make up the difference between your actual equity and 80% loan to value on the property. In reality, I have never seen this happen with long-term fixed loans. Nor do I understand how a mortgage company, with millions of loans, could actually keep track of such market changes.

Agreeably, these methods are not elegant or instant, but they work. They are also easy to understand and execute. More importantly, the buyer is not involved so these strategies do not require a willing buyer. As such, these techniques can be effectively used on all properties in both buyer and seller markets (hot or cold markets).

Financing for a Fixer-Upper

A *fixer-upper* is any property that could be identified by an appraiser or insurance adjuster as uninhabitable or not insurable. Some words of caution regarding the financing of a fixer-upper. Be aware that for financing purposes it makes a *big* difference whether the purchase is for an owner occupant or not. For owner-occupied financing, more flexibility exists and lending institutions such as the U.S. Department of Housing and Urban Development's Section offer loan programs for rehabs or fixer-uppers. When purchasing a fixer-upper for investment purposes, however, you typically need two forms of financing, acquisition money to buy the home, and then a second loan to do the actual repairs and make the improvements. Typically, you *cannot* use conventional financing to buy these properties if they are non-owner occupant purchases. If it is a non-owner occupied purchase, you typically must fund the construction part separately, then refinance the property when the work is complete to obtain conventional loan terms. For those of you that partake in these activities, it may be helpful to understand why financing for these situations is so restrictive. In a word, *homeowners' insurance*. Typically, no insurance company will provide property and casualty insurance on a dwelling that is uninhabitable or has been vacant for a long period. Without insurance on your asset, no lender will provide conventional financing.

Money Back at Closing

Some final words on obtaining money back at closing from the purchase of investment property. Although much flexibility exists with owner-occupied purchases, for non-owner-occupied investment property purchases using conventional financing, it is typically not possible for a buyer to leave the closing table with cash. There is only one way (currently) that I know of where you can receive some money back at closing from the seller. Under the current Fannie Mae and Freddie Mac guidelines, a seller is allowed to pay some of the buyer's closing costs. The actual amount depends on the state's lending rules, but is typically capped at around 5%. Closing costs include things like credit reports, appraisals, application fees, attorney fees, and taxes. If you enter into any type of agreement with the seller where the sale price is artificially raised and the seller plans to give you cash at closing, be cautious. Unless all agreements are captured in writing, they are often not enforceable.

Obviously if you obtain 100% financing on a property and you get the seller to pay the closing costs, then you can walk away with at least the amount of the closing costs. Otherwise, the only way I am aware of to get cash back from closing is when you refinance and do a cash-out refinance on a property you own.

Owner versus Non-Owner Occupied Financing

When you buy investment property it is typically financed as non-owner occupied. In such cases you will pay a higher interest rate than you would with owner-occupied purchases. The typical bump for a non-owner occupied investment property is $3/_8\%–1/_2\%$ added to your interest rate. Another difference between owner and non-owner occupied loans is the down payment requirement. For non-owner occupied investment properties, the equity requirement is usually 20–30%. In contrast to these non-owner investment loans, we all know what great deals are out there for owner-occupied conventional financing, where 100% financing is becoming the norm. Although usually not applicable, there is a great opportunity for getting low rates and financing terms if you are willing to live in a rental property you are buying for a minimum of six months. In this way, your loan may qualify as an owner-occupied loan.

Commercial Financing

The previous discussions have applied largely to conventional financing on small apartment buildings up to four units. If an apartment building has five or more units, a commercial loan is usually required. Banks often use the terms *commercial loans* and *major loans* interchangeably. The same loan officers who make the commercial loans for the bank also make the major loans. Major loans include not only commercial loans, but also land development loans and residential subdivision construction loans. Commercial loans may be amortized and have the look and feel of a conventional loan, but the key distinction is that the interest rates cannot be fixed for the term of the loan. Typically a balloon payment becomes due before the term expires, like after five, seven, or ten years. Because of this balloon feature, commercial loans follow the prevailing (short-term) interest rates and not necessarily the long-term (bond) rates. As we learned in the previous chapter, because of the balloon feature of the commercial loan, the profitability (and value) of commercial real estate is more driven by the prevailing interest rates. A sharp increase in interest rates around the time when your loan becomes due means you will likely need to refinance at a much higher interest rate, which of course cuts into your cash flow. For these reasons, buying property that can be financed with conventional loans (1–4 unit buildings) poses the least risk to the private investor.

Summary

- The type of loan you choose dictates your cash flow and thus affects your profitability.

- Conventional loans are the loans familiar to most homeowners, where the interest rate can be fixed for the term of the loan, typically fifteen or thirty years; these loans are available for single-family homes, duplexes, triplexes, and quadraplexes (1–4 units).

- Conventional loans are available for both owner-occupied and non-owner occupied investments; a non-owner mortgage will have a slightly higher interest rate ($^3/_8$ to $^1/_2$%) than a property that is owner-occupied.

- If an apartment building has five or more units, a conventional loan is not possible and usually a commercial loan is required.

- Commercial loans can be fixed for extended periods, but unlike a conventional loan, commercial loans typically have balloon payments where the total becomes due before the term is up.

- Due to the interest rate risk associated with commercial loans, buying property that can be financed with conventional loans (1–4 units) poses the least risk to the private investor.

- If you borrow more than 80% LTV on conventional loans, you have to pay private mortgage insurance.

- Cash-out refinancing is easy to apply and can be used to obtain cash at closing from existing investment property.

MAKING THE OFFER AND TAKING OVER

9

Having established that the property has a positive cash flow, is priced at market value, and is likely to appreciate, you are close to making an offer. One important thing remains before making your offer, and that is the inspection of the units. In most cases, there are two inspections you will need to make, one before the negotiations begin, which you will do yourself, and a second after you are under contract and before you actually close the deal, during what is commonly called the *due diligence period*. The first inspection is largely to find out whether it is a go, and if so, what it will cost you to get the units in shape. If things progress and you end up under contract, a final inspection should be performed. The purpose of the final inspection is to go through everything with a fine-toothed comb and ensure there are no sink holes, radon traps, termite damages, mold problems, or the like, and anything you may have missed the first time through. These inspections are typically performed by a professional in the home inspection business. This final inspection during the due diligence period gives you the option to back out of the deal if need be.

Pre-Offer Inspections

The purpose of the *pre-offer inspection* is to identify all major repairs and judge what is necessary to bring the units into rent-ready condition. You will need to walk through *all* the units and check the ceilings, walls, doors, floors, and windows carefully. You need to crawl—if necessary—through the crawl space and otherwise inspect the foundation of your proposed purchase. Look for rotted wood, leaky or old roofs, determine the age of the furnace, air conditioning, water heaters, and other appliances if the units are older. Attached in Appendix D is an example inspection form I use as a guide. I recommend, however, that you find a form that is specific to your region and property type. I have brought these forms or other checklists with me when I inspect and I am often distracted from the task at hand. It is hard to concentrate when the seller and/or tenants are standing beside you. My recommendation therefore is to bring another person with you. As you will be having a professional inspection done before you close the deal, your *primary* goal at this point should be to assess the *rentability* of the units. If the carpet or vinyl needs replacing and the place needs painting, make note of this. Take measurements of the room sizes so you can calculate costs later. If faucets need changing because they are old, or there are obvious repair items, make note of this as well. Check everything for proper operation. Check that doors close and latch, faucets run, toilets flush, and windows go up and down. Look at the units with the eyes of a prospective renter as well as a home inspector. You can dictate to your partner to ensure you capture most of your observations. If you can't entice a spouse or friend to come along, another good technique is to buy a small cassette recorder and put it in your pocket. The seller or Realtor will probably think you have a screw loose when you start talking to yourself, but it is a good way to capture all the repairs, carpet dimensions, etc., that will be needed. After you have left the property, check the inspection form and make notes of the items you missed. If you have missed major areas, you can request another visit to fill in the gaps. Your job is to find things that need to be repaired or updated at your expense. These are the items that were *not* part of your cash flow calculations and it is therefore imperative you uncover them before you commit to the negotiation phase of the deal. The list doesn't mean you will find everything. In fact, unless you are a trained and licensed contractor or inspector, you can't know everything to look for. That's why the professional inspection comes in later, after the offer is accepted.

Make-Ready Cost Estimates

If you have based your cash flow calculations on market rents and the actual rents are *below* market due to deferred maintenance, you need to estimate the cost required to bring the units up to standard. Owners usually sell when deferred maintenance mounts up and they get wind that all their long-term tenants are moving out. You, as the new owner, however, will be the last one to find this out. You need to *assume* that the tenants *will* move out, and therefore you need to calculate what it would cost to get the vacant units in the shape required to obtain the market rents. Pay particular attention to the costs associated with new carpet, new paint, and *especially* if new baths or kitchens are required. These are costly repairs to a new property owner. Look at the expense tables in Appendix B to come up with the cost of the *make ready*. Better yet, obtain repair estimates from a local handyman. I often arrange for another visit where I bring a contractor or handyman with me. He or she can then provide you with a written turn-key price on what it would cost to make all the repairs you identified in your pre-offer inspection. Get these estimates in writing as they will become important later when it comes time to negotiate.

Once you have tallied everything up, you have all the information needed to proceed to the negotiation phase. Be careful though. Before entering into this stage of the process you must mentally prepare yourself for the negotiations ahead.

Be Prepared to Walk

You are now ready to make the offer and get the deal done. The biggest and most profound mistake people make at this point is getting emotionally attached to the deal. You have read that you shouldn't get attached to the deal. You have done well up to this point, but now you succumb. Do not imagine yourself with this property. You must remain completely detached from the deal until the signatures are in place and the deed transfer is complete. This is not easy. The truth is, every investor gets emotionally involved at this point. If we weren't involved emotionally at some level, we would be buying mutual funds instead of investing in real estate. In any event, this part of the transaction requires you to put your emotions aside. The way I approach this stage of the business is by mentally convincing myself that I will *not* get the property throughout the negotiation. I assume someone will jump in at the last moment, bid the property up, and I will have to move on to the next one. Whatever (mental) technique you choose, be sure it works and make sure you are capable of walking if you have to. If you end up finding out the roof needs replacing and the seller isn't willing to work with you, be prepared to say no and move on. Be very polite and explain your reason, but decline. If you find out the seller misrepresented something, be prepared to pass on those deals as well.

Offer to Purchase Forms

Providing everything goes well and you actually are ready to make an offer, you will need the appropriate real estate forms. Whether you are working with a buyer's agent or not, be sure to use the National Association of Realtors' (NAR) *Offer to Purchase Contract* for your state. If you are working with a buyer's agent, he or she can supply the forms and help you fill them out. If you are working alone, most seller's agents are very helpful and will fill out the forms per your instructions. If you are unsure about how to complete any sections, ask the closing attorney or escrow agent you will be using. Typically these NAR forms are weighted heavily in favor of the buyer, so don't worry, there are already sections that cover items such as: wood-eating insects, inspections, repairs, property disclosures, personal property, closing expenses, and financing. If you find something illegitimate, or the inspection uncovers something, you can easily back out of a deal. This is why it is important to use the official realtor-provided forms. Do not bother with contracts obtained from real estate books, courses, or the Internet. Unless you are a lawyer, and even if you are, there is no need to reinvent the wheel. These official NAR forms are buyer bullet-proof. The many offer to purchase forms provided in real estate books mislead novice investors into thinking they need to hand-craft their contract. In reality, you just need to request and complete forms used by your local or state realtor association.

The Offer

In preparing your offer, an important decision right off is when to set your closing date. I usually place the closing date for thirty to forty-five days from the offer date. This usually gives you more than enough time to arrange for financing and take care of all the other details. Another important clause is regarding your right to inspect the property prior to closing. In very hot markets sellers can get away with selling their properties "as is." In these cases the buyer waives his or her right to an inspection. Another tactic used in such *seller markets* is having an inspection done for *information only*. Essentially this means you have the right to perform an inspection, but the seller will not pay for any repairs. This is okay because as long as you have not waived your right to a professional inspection, you can still back out of the deal if an inspection uncovers something you are not willing to accept.

There is always a section for comments in these offer to purchase contracts. Be sure to write a note making the offer good for *only* 24–36 hours. For example, simply write: "Offer good until 5 p.m. Friday." If the seller's agent says, "I think they are out of town," or "I don't know if I can get the paperwork to them that quick," just ignore it. Tell the seller's agent that you have reduced your search down to two proper-ties and you need an answer quickly because if this deal falls through, you need to move on to the next one. We are no longer in an age where marathon runners transfer paperwork from town to town. We have had offers faxed back to us at a hotel in Florida while on vacation (I could barely get my wife to sign that one). If the sellers are serious players, you will hear back. If they are not, you need to know that too. Make them sweat but make them answer. Time passing is *never* to the advantage of the buyer. Tell them you have another house and you can't float two offers and therefore you need a quick answer. Just be aware that if the twenty-four-hour period expires, and no counteroffers have been made in writing, that contract is then invalid. As soon as buyer and seller agree upon a price, make the change on the contract and get the sellers to sign as soon as possible. Always ensure both husband and wife sign if the property is jointly owned. In such cases, a single signature is non-binding until the second one is added.

Disclosure Forms

Your offer to purchase contract will have a box to check stating that you have (or have not) received a property disclosure form. If you are working with a buyer's agent, he or she will place a great emphasis on obtaining such a disclosure from your seller. These forms are now required by the National Realtor Association. In principal, they require the seller to disclose any deficiencies to any prospective buyers. In practice, however, this rarely occurs. I have seen disclosure forms where every category on the form is checked with no representation. I knew for a fact this particular building was termite-ridden and the structural integrity was greatly compromised. Was the (local) owner aware of this? I most definitely think so. The last time I drove by there were cement bags piled ten feet high in preparation for pouring new footers to replace the wood joists. Did the seller disclose any of this to the buyer? No. My final recommendation about disclosure forms is to request them, but place no value on them.

Earnest Money

Regardless of the purchase contract you decide to use, you will need to provide an earnest or good-faith deposit upon submitting your written offer. The purpose of the *earnest deposit* is to show your level of commitment. *Earnest deposit* amounts can vary widely but a typical deposit is 1–2% of the sale price. If the seller has a realtor, the seller's agent will hold the money until closing, at which time it is credited back to you. If the seller does not have a realtor, you can either give him or her the money directly, or alternatively you can have the deposit reside with a neutral third party, such as your closing attorney or escrow agent. Offering large earnest deposits sends a strong commit-ment signal, and can be used by the buyer to help leverage a deal. It is also very risky. Offer to purchase contracts are very specific about how and when earnest deposits are dispersed if the deal falls through. If you back out of the deal and there is no contractual contingency, you may very well lose that money. For these reasons I recommend never giving the earnest deposit directly to the seller or the seller's agent. Although it is customary to use the seller's agent as a third party, I often request that the closing attorney receive it. Given the many things that can upset a real estate deal, I also offer very low earnest deposits (as low as I can get away with) such as $500–$1000. This way, if anything goes wrong and I want out of the deal, I won't lose thousands of dollars. Obviously, the seller wants the opposite, so you will need to sweeten the deal by having a short closing period, good conventional financing, or some other incentives.

Be Careful of Contract Exclusions

We have recommended always using your local NAR offer to purchase contract. Be very wary if the seller or seller's agent is using any other type of contract or if the seller's agent has excluded certain sections from the NAR forms. If you are purchasing residential property that can be purchased with conventional financing (1–4 units), the most important section for buyers is the clause that states, "Buyer must be able to obtain *conventional* financing." The important term here is "conventional", and be wary because some seller's agents will remove this clause. If you are depending on obtaining a long-term fixed conventional loan (without a balloon payment) you need to ensure this clause is present. Without this clause, the seller can hold you to the deal, even if you are unable to get financing. We once bought a property with two single-family homes on a single lot. At the last minute we discovered that because of this, we could not obtain conventional financing. We had to finance this property with a commercial loan, amortized over twenty years, with a five-year balloon payment due.

Closing the Deal

As far as strategies for closing the deal, there are countless books on this subject alone. With so much expert advice already available, I will only present my top level view on how to effectively close a deal. In any real estate transaction, in order to make the deal go through, you need to determine the *drivers of your seller*. As an example, we once bought a duplex in dire need of renovation. The driver for the seller, and more importantly his wife, was that they wanted to rid themselves of the property with the least aggravation. They were willing to sacrifice a share of the profit in order to avoid dealing with the risks of an inspection or real estate agents. For that seller, then, our offer to purchase the property as is and a thirty-day closing fulfilled their needs. As part of our as is offer we required a five-day due diligence period where we could have the property inspected and back out of the deal for any reason. After this five-day period, if we did not decline in writing, the contract was binding. Another bit of advice: don't stall the negotiations over several thousand dollars. If the numbers work and you have verified the asking price as fair, and you and the seller are only several thousand apart, go ahead and close the deal. Your goal is to own the property, not lose it for $1.50 more per month in higher mortgage payments. This is especially true if it is a brand new listing. If the property has been on the market a while, e.g., over thirty days, never offer full price—rather, do some hard negotiating. Use the lower predictors of value that you obtained from doing your property value analysis to justify your lower offer.

Final Due Diligence and Taking Over

The pre-inspections are done, you are under contract, and the closing date looms. This is known as the *due diligence period*. Depending on how your contract was structured, there are likely some remaining contingencies, such as obtaining a post-offer (professional) inspection, viewing the leases, or arranging for financing. The *due diligence period* is typically a period of approximately five to ten days when you have the right of refusal if any of the contract contingencies are not met to your satisfaction. After this period, the contract becomes binding and it will become difficult to back out of the deal without losing your earnest deposit. If you have done your homework there should be no surprises here. If you are working with a buyer's agent, he or she will be of great value here, in ensuring all is in order for the closing. The first thing likely on your to-do list is making final inspections.

Post-Offer Inspections

The pre-offer inspections are necessary to determine the costs required to get the units into rent-ready condition. After buyer and seller have agreed to the terms of the sale, you are under contract, and the final inspections need to be performed. The purpose of this inspection is simply to be thorough and make sure you haven't missed any great structural flaw or some condition that would make you reconsider the deal. For this inspection you will want to enlist the help of a professional home inspection service. By and large the home inspection industry is poorly regulated, and the level of performance varies widely. In order to carry the title of home inspector in our state you need to be a member of the American Society of Home Inspectors (ASHI). Unfortunately, the training necessary to earn this title is minimal. The trade is improving, but you still need to be very vigilant when selecting your inspector. I would only hire inspectors who are also licensed as contractors in your state. Also try and find inspectors who have experience inspecting multifamily dwellings if that applies. Once you find a good inspector, just set him or her loose. You will receive a very detailed report on his or her findings. If there are no "show stoppers" you can proceed to closing. If there are any major flaws or items in need of repair, you can make a counteroffer or walk away from the deal. Once again, this will be *your* decision. Every market and seller is different. Some sellers will work with you to make repairs; others will refuse to pay a dime. The important thing is that the inspection gives you the right to back out of the deal if some major flaw is uncovered that you are not willing to pay to have repaired.

The Tenants

Essentially, closing on an investment property is no different than buying an owner-occupied house except that there are tenants to consider. So as part of the due diligence period, make sure you obtain copies of the leases. By having the leases, you will know how much to expect at closing from the seller regarding pro-rated rents and security deposits. Whether there is paperwork provided on the tenants or not, I usually create a form that the tenants can fill out answering simple questions like how much their rent is, how much their security deposit is, what items they own in the apartment, etc. Get a listing of autos they own so you don't get stuck with an abandoned vehicle. Also, it is very important to ask the question, "Do you have any other agreements or promises with the current landlord that I need to be aware of as the new owner?" You don't want a tenant telling you later that the security deposit was actually the last month's rent! Next, arrange for your homeowners' insurance and locate a good management company. I go into more detail later on how to actually shop and select these services. For the small fee they charge, management companies, in my opinion, are well worth it. You simply turn the leases and information over to them and your job is done with that aspect of the deal.

The previous sections have dealt more with the mechanics of the offer and closing stages of a real estate deal. In the following sections, we discuss different types of investment opportunities and how to recognize a good opportunity from one that may be high-risk.

Identifying Opportunities and Avoiding Problem Properties

Before making an offer, everyone always asks the seller why he or she is selling. Although I ask this question as well, I know there is usually only one reason why sellers sell—*money*. If the sellers are *not* making any money from the deal, the buyer needs to be especially cautious. You need to be very wary, for example, if the sellers have owned the property for only a few years or less. In such cases it is not only important to ask why they are selling, but you also need to verify their claims. If the reasons don't add up, or you are not convinced, just walk away and move on to the next one. This is especially true if the seller would be realizing a loss after paying realtor fees. There are too many unforeseeable problems in this business to even hazard taking a chance. The property could flood every time it rains, or it may have a tenant who stopped paying rent. There may be building code violations. There could be a $15,000 sewer repair necessary that would not be revealed in any home inspection. The list is both endless and terrifying. We once bought a property that had a well-worn path through the yard. We only noticed the trail after we took possession. We had hoped it was a deer trail, but given the inner-city surroundings, it was not likely. After just several weeks, the first tenant called and complained about vagrants using the yard as a pass-through. It eventually cost us $1,800 in fencing and a year-long battle with the attorney of the neighboring lot to solve the problem. You can't always avoid such misfortunes, but if the seller is taking a loss on the sale, and there is no good (verifiable) explanation as to why he or she is selling, be on guard. In such cases, you are usually better off just moving on to the next deal. There are too many safe opportunities out there to take a risk with any opportunity that hints of fraud.

If you know what to look for, you can minimize your risk of buying a problem property and maximize your chances of making a good investment. The following list summarizes seller situations that usually offer a good buying opportunity with minimal risk.

- The sellers are the original owners and want to retire from the rental property business.

- The sellers have owned the property long enough so they are making a *good* gain versus what they paid.

- The sellers are absentee (out-of-state) landlords and the property has poor management and/or vacancy.

- The sellers are trading up after several years' equity to another rental property or vacation property.

- The sellers need the equity for a family emergency (this is harder to verify).

The wrong properties to buy are simply properties that *do not* have any of the characteristics stated above. This list is not intended to be comprehensive and exclusive. If you are presented with a unique reason why the sellers are selling for a loss, *and* you can verify that reason as legitimate, you can still proceed with the deal. These properties, however, should be the *exception,* not the rule.

The Rehab Property

You have identified a good property to buy. The sellers are retiring from the business and selling the duplex they have owned for the last twenty years. Things look good from the curb, and then you finally get to see the inside. The walls are crumbling, the kitchen vinyl is split, and the carpets are shot. What should you do? Typically these situations rarely end up profitable for the new owner. When properties require major repairs and renovations, there is only one way this type of transaction can work. Calculate how much it would cost to get the units into rent-ready condition. You may need a contractor to walkthrough the units for this. If you can buy the property for market value less the cost of renovation, you may want to consider going forward with the offer. If you decide to go ahead, you have two choices. One is to pay the extra cash up front to make the repairs (this requires a lot of cash out-of-pocket). The other option, if you have fair to good credit, is to obtain a construction loan at a local bank to cover the property loan *plus* any planned renovation costs. In this way, you can obtain a cash advance at closing for the additional renovation costs. Then after six to twelve months, and after all the work is done, you can refinance and pay off the construction loan in full. If this is well executed, you can end up owning a fully renovated building for less than market price with less than 20% down. The following example is representative of this approach. We were interested in owning a duplex in a neighborhood close to us that we targeted as a high-growth area. The problem was that no duplexes had sold in this area for over five years and there weren't any units currently available. We sent out letters to all the owners soliciting a realtor-free sale, and an owner eventually contacted us. The duplex was beautiful from the outside; new driveways, new furnaces, and new roof with gutter guards. The market rents for the area were $650–$695, but his units were rented for $550 and $575. We thought this to be odd, until we walked inside. The ceilings were stained with leaks, the carpet and vinyl ruined; in short, both apartments required full renovations. We had a contractor go through and he offered a turn-key renovation of $20,000 for both apartment units. At the time, the duplexes in the area were estimated to have a market value of approximately $180,000. We sent the seller a letter itemizing our projected renovation costs, along with estimated loss of rents for the two to three months required to complete the work. We offered him $150,000 and promised a short closing period. We also offered to buy the property as is (we had already inspected it at this point). He eventually took our offer. His driver was unloading a headache and we gladly provided that service. After two months the renovations were complete and the building was rented for $700 per side. After six months we refinanced and paid off the construction loan. Although the cash flow for this property was actually predicted to be slightly negative, we decided to proceed anyway. Why? Remember that our original expense factor used in our DCR estimate was 45%. Because we now own fully renovated units with a new roof, furnace, siding, and driveways, we predict lower expenses for the foreseeable future. Another plus on this deal was that the area has an excellent record of appreciation and should now benefit from a new mall being built down the street.

I provide this example only to illustrate that there are many ways to make a deal work. Be aware, though, that there are several factors that had to work in our favor here. For one, there is an interest rate risk. If rates increase during the renovation period, your profits may be less than predicted due to unplanned higher monthly payments. Also, you need to be absolutely certain the construction costs do not exceed estimates. The risk of the appraisal coming in lower than market value is negligible. If you did your homework regarding your estimates of comparable market values, the appraisal should come in as expected. In reality, mortgage brokers are usually more flexible with refinance appraisals and try to accommodate the customer, if at all feasible.

The Mismanaged Property

Perhaps the best opportunity to make money in the real estate business is to buy properties that are selling for below market because of low rents or vacancies due to poor or absentee management. It is important, however, to differentiate between management issues and extensive deferred maintenance. If rents are low due to old plumbing or heating or the need to renovate a kitchen or bath, there is usually little value to be had. What you are looking for are units that can be brought up to rent-ready condition with minor repairs. You want to limit expenses to the cost of new carpet, vinyl, paint, and cosmetic repairs. If you are lucky, you may even find rents that are below market with units in good shape. This typically happens in buildings with long-term tenants where the rents haven't been increased in years. This is often due to absentee land-lords, or older owners where the property is paid off and they are not aware of current market rents. In these cases you can buy the prop-erty for below market due to the low rents and simply raise rents after you take possession. In some cases the tenants will simply pay the new rent knowing they have had a good deal for many years. In most cases, however, they will move out. This is fine, as you can then go in and clean, make minor repairs as necessary, replace carpet, vinyl, etc., and rent the units at the higher market prices. Overall it is a win-win situation as you now have a property that is probably worth more than you paid for it. The only word of caution is that you need to be financially prepared in the event the tenants decide to move out. You also need to allow at least several months for completing the required work and getting the units leased. Due to the prolonged vacancy, be sure to factor in loss of rents, adver-tising, and *considerable* utility costs during this make-ready phase.

Summary

- In most cases there are two property inspections you will make, one before the offer, where you assess the condition and estimate the cost of any make-ready repairs that may be needed, and a second inspection after you are under contract, during what is commonly called the due diligence period.

- When making your offer, be sure to use the National Association of Realtors' (NAR) *Offer to Purchase Contract* for your state.

- Be alert for any excluded sections in your contract, especially concerning your right to conventional financing for the purchase of one- to four-unit family apartments.

- A good opportunity to make money is to buy properties that are in good condition and are selling for below market because of low rents and/or vacancies due to poor or absentee management.

ADVERTISING AND RENTING

10

Whether you choose to use a management company or not, you must be very proficient at advertising and filling your vacancies. If your advertising methods are not effective, you will quickly end up in big financial trouble. The methods that you use to solicit tenants therefore are important, and knowing where to concentrate your efforts is critical. The POMS survey provided valuable information as to which advertising methods work best. As shown in the following figure, the most effective form of advertising when seeking new tenants is word of mouth. Apparently, keeping your tenants happy—and thus ensuring they recommend your apartments—is very important.

Methods of Adverting for New Tenants

Method	Total	1–4 Units	5–49 Units	>50 Units
Newspaper ads	61.9%	58.7%	66.8%	65.3%
Apartment guides	15.3%	8.6%	17.6%	52.3%
"For Rent" sign	51.4%	48.4%	57.1%	49.6%
Word-of-mouth referrals	75.1%	72.3%	76.7%	88.1%

Source: "Property Owners and Managers Survey" by U.S. Census 2000. Note: For some items in this table, the percentages are given only for the top categories and may not add to 100%.

The second most effective methods of advertising were newspaper ads and posting signs in front of your property. Although newspaper ads are a good way to bring in tenants, you will absolutely (trust me) go *broke* running newspaper ads for your vacancies. Ads in our metropolitan area newspaper average about $100 to get coverage for just one weekend. Typical vacancies in our area can often run as long as three months, so advertising in your local newspaper can get expensive very quickly. Interestingly, according to the POMS study, the use of "For Rent" signs is nearly as effective as newspaper advertising. Signs, in fact, are so important and cheap (free), that I dedicate a whole section on how to effectively use them

"For Rent" Signs

By far, signs provide your best value and return when advertising your vacancies. You therefore need to understand how to fully exploit this technique. In our area, we receive about the same number of calls from our signs as we do from running a newspaper ad. Quite interestingly, we later discovered this *hit rate* of signs versus newspaper ads, was, in fact, as expected based upon the POMS survey results presented earlier. In short, signs are your best bet. This is why I place great emphasis on buying your properties in high-visibility areas, if at all possible. Rental properties on high-traffic road frontage rent easily when compared with apartments that are buried six turns into a neighborhood. You will spend a small fortune in advertising for these low-exposure properties as compared with poking a free sign in the ground on a high traffic-exposure property.

> NOTE:
> If you end up signing on a new tenant before the old tenant moves out, the period after the old tenant moves out and new tenant move-in is not considered a vacancy. This is rather known as a *turnover*.

If you do place ads in the paper, and you are with a management company, be sure to include your phone number in the ad. This gives you the opportunity to talk to prospective tenants. By talking directly with prospective tenants, you are also gathering valuable data. I keep a book where I write down all the tenant contacts. About thirty days later, if the unit is still not rented, I call them back. I am most interested in learning *why* they didn't choose our apartments. Listen to this feedback, as it is important. Your properties may need updating, or may be missing that second bathroom everyone is looking for now. Stay tuned in to tenant needs. This is critical in order to maintain maximum occupancy at market rents.

Using a Realtor

Although our management company was extremely competent in many areas, they were terrible at keeping our units at maximum occupancy. We found a rather clever way, however, to have the best of both worlds—we hired a local real estate company to rent our units. They have a huge local presence and essentially dominate the relocation market in our area. As part of their service, they conduct the move-in inspection and write up a very comprehensive lease. At this point, we just turn the tenancy over to our management company, and mission accomplished. It is expensive, as we pay one month's rent for the lease-up fee, but it's cheap when compared to paying for several months' vacancy and utility bills. We would go with this company as a permanent management company, but they require an 8% management commission, which is too high for us.

Internet Advertising

If the POMs survey were updated, it would no doubt add a category for Internet advertising. The Internet can be a great advertising tool for the right properties. Internet advertising is most effective when you are targeting a demographic that utilizes the Web to locate apartments, such as students and middle- to high-income households. The Internet is a less effective means of advertising for affordable housing. If you own several apartments or more it may be worth your effort to set up your own website. It is actually quite simple. If you are just starting out with website publishing, you can contact your Internet provider for guidance. They often offer a free web page. Although traffic to such a site may be limited, it is a convenient source of advertising information for prospective tenants. After you gain some experience with a free website, it may be worth your efforts to set up your own website with your own URL, for example **www.mynameproperties.com**. Typically, this will cost under a hundred dollars to set up. The monthly charges are also minimal. Such websites are a convenient place to store information. You can maintain forms, records, lease expiries, pictures, and property descriptions, all in one central location. You will probably need to buy a book on setting up your own website and also purchase a copy of a web publishing software, such as Microsoft Front Page. After setting up your website you can register it with major search engines to increase traffic to your site.

Perhaps an easier (and cheaper) option to gain Internet exposure is to take advantage of websites that already have high traffic of prospective tenants. Many of these Internet websites where you can post classified ads are free. For example, websites such as Craigslist (**www.craigslist.org**) target local areas, allow free or extremely inexpensive ads, and have high traffic. Your listing description can be fairly lengthy (if you desire), and you can even include photos. It's also helpful to see how your unit compares to others in the area in terms of rent and amenities. To locate the appropriate Internet vehicle in your area, just perform some simple searches using the appropriate key words. You will quickly discover the websites that dominate the rental advertising market in your area.

Student Rentals

As stated earlier, signs are a good way to bring in tenants. This is most true with student rentals. In addition to signs, make sure you use the student newspaper, as this is your best bet for cheap, effective advertising. Posting flyers on bulletin boards near the student union, bookstore, or library can also be productive. Whereas Internet advertising is not very effective for low-income housing, for student housing it is very important. Being students, they tend to use the Internet for everything, and finding an apartment is no different. During the student rental season, we rent four out of every five of our units from our website or other local Internet advertising sites. Here is where having your own website is useful, as you can just list the URL address in newspapers or flyers to lead students to the information.

Advertise at Market Rent

Assuming you get good coverage by signs, newspaper ads, realtors, the Internet, flyers, or all of the above, you need a way to determine whether your rent is too high, too low, or just right (*market rent*). In general, if you are getting a lot of showings and no one is signing on, there is likely some other problem instead of price. If you are getting no calls or activity whatsoever, chances are you are advertising above market rent for what you are describing in your ads. Most tenants will not look at higher-priced apartments with the idea that they will negotiate if they like it; rather, they will simply focus on the lower price range. It is therefore essential you get good feedback from tenants that have seen your apartment but decided to live elsewhere. If your units are not renting, you need to understand the reason. At least then you have the information necessary to correct the problem. If that corrective action is not feasible in your case, you must either live with the longer vacancies or lower your rent to compensate for its shortcomings.

Rent Concessions and Keeping Tenants

Although offering rent concessions to attract and keep tenants is common, I would advise against it. Rather than using concessions, do your research and find out the reason your units are not renting. If two baths are required and you only have one bath, then either lower your rent or put in the required bath. In order to see what techniques have been successfully used by our fellow landlords to attract and retain tenants, we refer once again to the POMS study. The following figure summarizes the most effective methods to attract and retain tenants.

Method Type	Total	1–4 Units	5–49 Units	>50 Units
Rent concessions	27.2%	28.1%	24.2%	25.9%
Increasing maintenance	40.5%	38.5%	46.6%	50.4%
Upgrading units	46.5%	44.4%	52.0%	59.9%
Other improvements	41.1%	38.8%	46.6%	62.1%

Source: "Property Owners and Managers Survey" by U.S. Census 2000. Note: For some items in this table, the percentages are given only for the top categories and may not add to 100%.

NOTE:
The use of rent concessions to fill a vacancy is poor practice. We find that such concessions only attract short-term tenants and another vacancy and make-ready. Since vacancy and make-ready costs are your biggest expenses as a property owner, it is better to wait until you find a tenant who really wants to live in your apartment.

Perhaps surprisingly, providing rent concessions to attract tenants actually ranked the lowest as a technique used to attract or retain tenants. Nearly half the respondents agreed that increasing maintenance, upgrading units, or, in general, items that can be classified as making improvements ranked the highest. The take-home message is that if you are sitting on a vacancy for prolonged periods and you are asking market rent, you need to find out what improvements must be made to attract tenants and keep them. In the long run, this may be a better option than simply lowering the rents. You need, however, to price out the needed changes and then perform a comparative analysis to calculate how long it will take to pay off these improvements with the new higher (market) rents. After performing such analyses, you will often find that adding on that bathroom is not financially sound after all, in which case you just go with the option of lowering the rent.

Summary

- The most effective ways to advertise according to the POMS study is by word of mouth, followed closely by newspaper ads and using well-placed signage.

- Internet advertising can be a very effective form of advertising, especially for student rentals.

- Newspaper ads are prohibitively expensive and no more effective than using signs, and therefore should be your last choice.

- According to the POMS study, keeping your units in good shape and responding to tenants' needs is the most effective way to retain tenants, maintain market rents, and minimize turnover.

- If you are getting no calls or activity on your property, chances are you are asking above market rent for what you are describing in your ads.

- If you are getting a lot of showings and no one is signing on, there is likely some other problem besides price.

Managing Your Investments

11

You have just closed the deal and it is time to take over as the new owner. Whether you choose to manage your properties yourself or hire a management company, *how* you manage your properties can make the difference between success and failure. This is especially true in today's competitive markets where cash flow margins can be razor thin when starting out. After ten years, when rents are up, you can afford to be a hands-off manager. For new property owners though, you must actively mange your investment to ensure that the profit margins are as good as they can be. You need to become interested and knowledgeable about things like the types of leases you can use, how to screen tenants, deciding pet policies, how to advertise to attract tenants, when and how to handle the dispersing of security deposits, how late payments and delinquent rents are dealt with, how and if a collection agency is used for back rents owed, etc. All these questions and more are now your concern.

Should I Manage Myself?

If you already have a day job that supports your real estate investing, there is only one correct answer here. You should hire a management company. The small fee you will pay on commission is well worth having someone remind a tenant each month about late payments, or tracking down bad checks, or dealing with evictions. If you are self-employed, retired, unemployed, or otherwise have the time, then by all means go ahead and manage the units yourself. If you do this, though, be sure to properly educate yourself on landlord law. Read as many good books on the subject as you get your hands on. For the rest of us, however, we will need to concentrate our efforts on managing the management company. This being said, despite all your calculations and planning, a sure way to a negative cash flow is *not* managing every decision your management company makes. Let them collect the rent, send late payment letters, track down lost checks, and listen to all the complaints. Let them issue keys, take applications, show properties, and get leases signed. Let them answer every call. All these activities are useful and essential to you but they all have one thing in common: they do not affect your bottom line and they do not require any decisions from you. As soon as *you* receive the call about a necessary repair, *that* is a decision juncture, and requires your careful thought and correct course of action. I have worked intimately with many companies and they have only one interest at hand, and that is avoiding confrontation with the tenant. This being said, there are actually degrees of competence within management companies. I will follow with a list of the key areas of management that need to be micromanaged. These are also the areas you can query a prospective management company about. What you will likely find is that some management companies rank high in certain areas, like collecting rents, but fail miserably in other areas, like in the qualifying of tenants. In short, their concern as a management company is keeping the tenants happy, often at your expense. The owners won't be the ones hauling the management company into court for dipping into a security deposit to cover a damaged carpet. Given the choice, your management company will likely take the conservative position of *normal wear and tear* and therefore charge you for the damage, and not the tenant. Because of these issues, you need to understand precisely where the law lies so you can be an active participant in the management of your properties. Dealing with tenants and management companies is definitely a case of "what you don't know *will* hurt you." There are situations where such micromanagement may not be necessary. As mentioned previously, if your properties are paid off or your cash flow is great, you may not care about the loss of profits due to inefficient management. Or, you may be lucky in life, and have found the perfect management company. We, however, are still looking.

> **NOTE:**
> Ensure that the management company you are about to hire has a well-defined program of "triggers" for late payments. In my experience, companies that send out owners checks by the middle of the month nearly always have a well-disciplined system in place culminating in eviction proceedings by the thirteenth to the fifteenth of the month. This isn't to say that all companies that send out statements at the end of the month will have poor rent collection policies. It is only more likely that this will be the case.

Screening Tenants

It is of the utmost importance to screen tenants carefully. Why? Remember the demographics shift that was discussed earlier—as rents shift downward, landlords must develop new strategies to protect themselves against a different class of tenants. All management companies claim they check previous rental references and perform credit checks. A credit check, however, is meaningless unless someone actually reads, interprets, and rates the tenant's credit. And a rental reference is meaningless unless there is a minimum requirement set, like verification of a prior rental history. For this reason, only consider management companies that actually use tenant databases or otherwise have access to the credit bureaus. These tenant databases maintain a record of "dead beat" tenants as well as responsible ones. Any eviction filed anywhere in the country becomes part of a database. If a landlord reports a tenant for unpaid rents, the information will be in a database. So in short, ensure that either you, or the company you propose to use, utilizes these databases and do not rent to a tenant with less than a spotless record of paying rents. Let some other less scrupulous landlord inherit that problem tenant.

Prior References

Do not, I repeat, *do not* accept a tenant with no previous rental history. The story of, "Oh, I just moved away from home," or "I just left my husband," should fall on deaf ears. Yes, they may be telling you the truth, but they still haven't proven whether they can pay the rent on time, every month, year after year. Don't worry, they will find a place to live, just not in your apartment. In fact, do not rent to any tenant without at least two prior addresses with good references. If you follow these basic rules, you will find your tenants are responsible and upstanding citizens that take care of your units, pay rent on time, and, in general, contribute to your bottom line in a very positive way. If you do not manage this aspect of your business, you will forever be dealing with someone else's problem. You will be paying court costs and suffer vacancies due to evictions. You will be left with mounds of trash and trashed units after the evicted tenants are gone. This brings me to my favorite topic, which is problem tenants and how to avoid them.

> NOTE:
> It is a good idea to include in your vacancy advertisement that rental applications and prior rental references are required. This will tend to keep away the problem tenants.

Problem Tenants

We once had a 62-year-old woman, a physical therapist, with good credit (we were told) but with no prior rental references. Against our better judgment, we succumbed to the management company's wishes and allowed her to move in. She called about minor repairs every other day for about three months straight. Most repair requests were, in fact, unfounded; it was almost as if she was forgetful at times. Being the responsible landlords we are, we responded to each request, and sent our handyman over every time she called. She paid her first month's rent on time, but the following two months, the rents came later and later. She eventually just stopped paying rent altogether after four months of tenancy. We finally evicted her and are still owed over $2,000 in back rents. The unit sat empty from November through June. This brings me to the two most important pieces of advice about managing delinquent tenants. First, as mentioned earlier, ensure your management company follows the law in your state *to the letter* for collecting delinquent rent. Have the manager describe in detail the eviction process and the company's role in the process. Make sure if the company is to be in court on the fifteenth to file for possession, that the company is vigilant about this. Second, never accept partial payment of rent. In order to understand why this is so, let me explain the process of eviction in our state—it is probably similar in other states. A late notice (should) be sent out by the seventh of the month. On the thirteenth, if the rent is not received, an eviction notice is filed where the tenant must show up in court ten days later to pay rent or possession for the unit will be filed. Then, after seven to nine days, a sheriff will perform the lockout and you will repossess the unit. The whole process takes about thirty days. A little-known fact to the landlord is that if the tenant shows up on the last day of the month and offers to pay $500 of the $700 rent owed for that month and you accept it, the entire eviction process must be started from the beginning (to collect the remaining $200 owed plus the next month's rent that the tenant probably won't pay). In this way, the tenants buy time and can continue to live in your unit, resulting in more losses to you. The lesson learned is this: Do not ever accept partial payment of rent, and do not ever stop the eviction process from moving forward until you have all money owed to you in hand, in the form of a certified check.

In our case, the woman stopped paying rent in October and we began eviction proceedings October 15. She came to us in November, five days before the sheriff lockout, with $750 (full month's rent) for October and half of November's rent. Although tempting, we refused the partial payment. Our management company said it was a mistake. They said we wouldn't see a penny if we didn't accept it. Maybe they were right. We do know that if we accepted the payment, we would need to start the eviction process all over again and delay the eviction for yet another month. The correct decision in our mind was to get rid of the tenant and move on with life. The delinquent debt was reported to the credit authorities and will remain a part of her credit history for a period of seven years. This is your best recourse for collecting owed rents and damages. We have received delinquent rents and damages owed as much as three years later. If a tenant with such an unpaid collection on his or her credit history wants to buy a new car or house, and is refused the loan based upon his or her poor credit, you will be surprised how quickly he or she will pay off that debt to clear his or her credit. What was the lesson learned from this experience? This particular tenant had no prior references. In fact, a brief investigation indicated that she was a repeat offender and our management company's screening policies were insufficient to protect us from this rogue tenant.

> **NOTE:**
> A direct consequence of strict tenant screening is that your units will stand vacant longer. This is because you are being more selective and are thus not allowing substandard tenants to occupy your units. This vacancy, however, is by far cheaper in the long run than the price you will pay when leasing to unqualified tenants.

Pets

Most books on landlording and managing rental properties make the claim that over 50% of Americans own pets, and therefore by excluding pets, you lose out on 50% of the possible tenant market. Since this is the *only* reason I could think of why I should allow pets, I decided to take the time to research the legitimacy of this claim. The first part of this statement I found to be correct. Indeed, well over 50% of Americans *do* own pets. But does 50% of the *tenant* population own pets? No, in fact, they do not. If you are a tenant faced with potentially moving every year, and faced with landlords who *overwhelmingly* do not allow pets, you are far less likely to own a pet. So when your management company invariably makes this argument to you—don't believe it. You will *not* be losing out on many potential tenants if you do not allow pets. Once this myth is dispelled, there are, in fact, very few good reasons to allow pets. The small increases in rent you can claim are insignificant when compared with the level of risk you expose yourself to. When that old lethargic poodle you permitted passes on and is replaced with a rottweiler, your problems have just escalated. Since your lease allowed a dog, don't think for a minute the tenant will check in first to see if it is okay to buy a puppy to replace Fru Fru. Additionally, these days, your landlord insurance policy will not allow a whole host of dogs. They won't advertise this small fact, but go ahead and ask them for a list of prohibited pets. They will promptly send you one. Nearly all companies will not allow dog breeds such as dobermans, chows, pit bulls, or rottweilers. I'll bet, however, that you didn't know the list also includes staffordshire terriers (aka pitt bulls), sharpeis, presa canarios, and dalmatians. These names may sound harmless enough as your manager describes the mutt as a sluggish, cage-trained family dog. When one of these bruisers, however, takes a piece out of an unannounced guest, your insurance *will not* cover the lawsuit about to be hung around your neck. In short, if you need to allow dogs, go by pictures, not names. Provide your manager with pictures of these disallowed pets so they do not try and rely on names he or she may not recognize. This still won't protect you from an unauthorized pet replacement due to a death or otherwise loss of existing pet. Don't get me wrong; I am not pet adverse. I grew up with many different pets. I just do not allow them in my units.

If you must allow pets, though, here are my rules. Cats are better than dogs, only when cats are not combined with a dog. Cats are territorial, and if threatened by the presence of another pet in the same household, they can be filthy. They have been known to spray and soil outside of their boxes in the presence of another unwelcome pet. If you have carpets and they are very old, then you may consider renting to pets. If you allow pets, ensure the lease specifies the exact type of pet permitted. Make it clear that no substitute is allowed. As I mentioned before, be sure you or your management company uses pictures to screen for allowed breeds of dogs. Be sure to collect a pet deposit. Check with local and state laws, but usually you can demand at least a half month's rent as a pet deposit. Do this. Do not collect a non-refundable pet fee. Management companies love these pet fees as they needn't be bothered with going after the tenants for any subsequent pet damages. As an owner, however, I don't like them. A fee paid in advance gives some tenants the feeling they have already paid for Fido to decorate the rug and it is therefore okay. A deposit, on the other hand, is better insurance the tenants will be more mindful of damages their pets may cause.

The Right Lease

I will not go into details about how to write a lease or provide some legal form that will get you in trouble. Many books will state that you do not need the kitchen sink in a lease agreement, rather just the important sections. I disagree. The advocates of such leases are obviously far removed from the day-to-day activities of managing their units. Landlording is the most unpredictable business there is because it deals with people. For this reason, you want a lease that covers every possible eventuality that is even remotely probable. Finding such a lease is actually very simple. You do not need to be creative here; rather, follow the lead of the National Association of Realtors (NAR). What you want is your home state's NAR lease. Just contact the local escrow agent or attorney you used for closing and ask if he or she can provide a lease. These leases are quite comprehensive and we have yet to have an incident that wasn't covered in these leases. You may have to visit a realtor, schmooze, or otherwise dig around until you find a copy. The point is to not reinvent the wheel and spend time trying to write your own lease.

Enforce It

You have probably heard the saying, "leases are made to be broken." You must always remember though, for every lease that is broken, a landlord has allowed it. Don't get me wrong, tenants will pick up and leave, acquire a disallowed pet, stop cutting their grass, or stop paying rent. You cannot and will not ever stop these occurrences. If you qualified all your tenants in a rigorous manner, you should experience such problems only infrequently. After all, you do have creditable, responsible tenants. In any event, you must be prepared. Ensure that you or your management company put some teeth behind the lease. By *teeth*, I mean that once the lease is violated, a letter is sent with an *action date* and *consequence* if the lease violation is not corrected by that date. Make sure your management company has the means and is willing to *exercise* the authority to uphold the lease, if the violation is not corrected. Make the management company show you a copy of the letters they have sent to verify their policies. Many companies will send letters, but when you read them there are really no consequences or deadlines in them; thus, they are largely ignored. This is so important to get right that I have dedicated the following section on how to deal with lease violations.

The Three Rules of Lease Enforcement

As soon as a tenant breaks the lease, pick up your lease and read the section that addresses the violation at hand. If you chose the NAR lease for your state, you will find the lease is very clear on most topics. Just enforce the lease—it is that simple. If you give an inch, you prolong the inevitable. If you are a friend of your tenant (not recommended) and he or she is down on his or her luck, be understanding, but explain that it is business, and therefore you have no choice but to uphold the lease. The key to obtaining results with delinquent tenants is writing letters that contain three components. These three components need to be in EVERY letter you send to a tenant about a lease violation.

1. Paraphrase the lease violation. ". . . Per your lease, section x, y, z, your ten-foot python must be removed . . ."

2. Set an action date. ". . . from your apartment by month, day . . ."

3. Have a consequence. " . . . if this doesn't occur by this date, we will proceed IMMEDIATELY with eviction proceedings and you will be responsible for all fees and expenses incurred in renting your unit per section x, y, z of your lease . . ."

Without providing written notice with these three components, you *will not* be successful at landlording. You will get gray hair listening, pleading, and negotiating, but you will not ever be successful at collecting lost rents, or ridding problem tenants with pets, drugs, or ten of their closest friends. You simply will not win at that game. Another final word of advice: sooner is *always* better than later. If you want to rid your property of a prohibited pet, allow days, not weeks. The longer you delay, the more creative your tenant will become and the harder of a battle you will face.

Repairs and Maintenance

Although the median expenditure for maintenance and repairs is 13–17% of gross rents, the actual *range* is quite large (see Appendix E). Your expenditures for repairs and maintenance is the largest, most important expense you need to control after your purchase and during management. For that reason, you must have a good, sound approach to taking care of the minor repairs. These repairs are to be differentiated from larger repairs or replacement items that may fall under *capital improvements*. Repairs and maintenance for tax purposes range from the minor repairs such as stopped garbage disposals, plumbing leaks, cleaning, and stuck windows to larger repairs, such as termite damages, driveway repairs, painting your units, etc. You need good systems in place to handle all of these repairs, from small to large. The following sections address how to handle both the small and large repairs in order to minimize this expense.

Handling Minor Repairs

Even though you have a management company, it is essential you find a good handyman for small repairs. If a management company has their own hired help to make these repairs, they are directly benefiting from your expenses. Most management companies, therefore, make most of their profits not by their management fees, but rather by catering to the tenants' every wish, at *your* expense. This is a good situation for the management companies but a bad situation for you and your cash flow. Even if the management company claims to subcontract this work and therefore does not profit from it, it will still be expensive if you go through them. Service calls range from $40 to $80, depending on which part of the country you live in.

Although there are exceptions to this rule, I suggest you just bypass the management company services by identifying a good handyman. Find someone who can do minor electrical, plumbing, appliance repair, carpentry, etc. This will save you hundreds and hundreds of dollars per year. We have a system where our management company just notifies us of the potential problem, then *we* decide the course of action (remember the management company's job is to do the busy work, not to *decide* about things that affect your bottom line). We (or our handyman) usually call the tenant and ask a few confirmatory questions. Is it a circuit breaker? Did you try this or that? If it sounds like a genuine repair, we then will authorize it. We have made up a one-page sheet where the work is recorded to simplify our records. The handyman has a stack of them. He then just mails the completed form to us and we pay him. We give him a set of keys as well so he can have access to the units. If you do give the keys out, ensure the tenants give a verbal "okay" for the handyman to enter if the tenants are not there.

We find that this type of system works best for us. Since the handyman works for you, you can get an honest answer about whether the garbage disposal had a fork in it (and is thus a tenant expense) or was truly just broken (and is therefore an owner expense). I like it, too, because I am able to control costs more effectively. I know I will receive the full check from our management company every month and I don't need to be surprised by that $200 faucet replacement.

If you opt for this method of handling repairs, or even if you don't, I would let the management company know you wish to be notified of all repairs greater than zero dollars. In this way, even if the management company does the repairs, you are at least aware of them. You can then request an estimate up front if there are large repairs, or request more information.

Painting

In addition to having a good handyman, you will also need a good, cheap, painter. The number one rule for painting your units is, "Do *not* yield to your management company's wish to repaint your unit every tenant turnover." If you follow my guidelines, you should only have to paint your apartments once every five to eight years.

Be sure the painter uses a *flat* sheen paint, not paints such as gloss, semi-gloss, egg shell, or matte. You do not have to use the usual boring, ceilingwhite color that management companies use. You may use beige or copper colors to add a little life to your units. If you stick to flat finishes, you will (nearly) always be able to match a color at a home improvement store using their electronic matching system. This way you can touch up the walls between tenancies and do not need to repaint whole walls and ceilings so often. The paints with sheens change with manufacturers, and even change within the same manufacturer over time. In this way, the paint companies ensure you must buy more paint to cover the entire room instead of just touching up the place. I found you can touch up walls using flat paints for up to ten years without even noticing the touch ups. On the other hand, you can buy the exact same paint one year later that is in egg shell sheen and it will leave a noticeable (sheen) difference. In order to get a match for a touch-up job, you (or the painter), only need to remove a quarter-sized piece of paint from the wall, and take it to a local home improvement store for an electronic match. Although there is really no need to save touch-up paint when using this system, I usually just dip a paint stick into the paint can, and after it dries you can label it with the paint information and unit. If you need touch-up paint at a later date you can either buy the exact paint again, or just get an electronic match from the paint stick. This way, you do not need to store the paints you will use for touch-ups. I prefer this method as opposed to storing umpteen cans of paint in my garage. Be sure your painter is okay with this touch-up philosophy. If he or she is accustomed to working with landlords, he or she will be. If you find your painter is always suggesting repainting the whole apartment, it is time to find a more accommodating painter.

Bigger Jobs

For any major plumbing, electrical, furnace, building, or structural problems you run into, I recommend hiring a professional. There is simply too much at stake regarding your property, as well as liability issues, to chance using a handyman unless your handyman is licensed in the trade. Fixing is okay for the handyman, but when *new* wiring or plumbing is required, it is best to ensure it is done by a licensed trade person. Get at least three bids and if (at least) two are not consistent, get another bid until you have a sense of what it should cost. Work only with a business that has worked with rental property owners often. They will all answer yes to this question, so be sure you verify this by asking for landlord references. You will find that workers who are accustomed to working with rental property owners get "in and out" quickly and keep things simple. They know how to schedule work with the tenants, obtain keys, and get things done. They know that landlords are impatient people but a good source of business so they tend to be very focused on getting the job done. Try your management company out first for leads in this area. When working with trades-people, never pay *any* money in advance. The credible tradesmen will never require it. I work with a concrete guy that will do $5,000 worth of work and only send the bill upon completion.

What is Really Necessary?

Before you spend a mountain of money for something that needs repair, you first need to carefully determine *exactly* what is needed to *correct* the problem. The following example will serve to illustrate this concept. We have a duplex with a very long concrete driveway. The driveway had an area where a tree root had broken the slab and pushed the concrete up about six inches where the tenant parked his car. The driveway was also cracked nearly everywhere and clearly needed replacement. We first removed the troublesome trees, which cost $970, so that future cracks could be prevented. The cost estimate to replace the driveway was $4,000. Since we had trouble renting this place, we decided to pay an extra $400 for an additional parking area where we could install a carport (cost of carport = $1,000). We had only owned this duplex for one year, so this was definitely an unwelcome expense. The first thing I did was calculate the cash flow numbers for this unit, and the reserve cash was simply not there. We then asked our concrete man about the possibility of just repairing it, and what that would cost. It turns out that a repair would cost $650. Furthermore, he went on to explain that it would probably last five years. This, in fact, was the correct course of action. This is the hardest thing for landlords to get their arms around. In short, *if it can be repaired for less than replacement, repair it!* The only exception to this rule is when the proposed improvements would increase the potential rent. But then you need to do the math. In our case above, we estimated that a carport may bring an extra $25 per month. The increased rents per year with a carport is $25 x 12 = $300 / year. With these numbers, the carport would take eighteen years to pay off all expenses ($4,000 (drive) + $400 (slab) + $1,000 (carport) ÷ $300 / year). I did not include the trees in this calculation as I had no choice but to remove them or the problem would continue. Since eighteen years far exceeds the useful life of a car port, this option is unattractive to me. Agreed, the repair option may be a waste of money, especially if I need to turn around in three to five years and replace the drive. But who knows, maybe I can fix it again in five years. Bottom line—this approach keeps me in a positive cash flow. The homeowner inside of me wanted to replace the driveway, but the landlord in me finally arrived at the right decision. I am now considering having just the additional parking pad added for $400, then adding the carport for $1,000. The carport, at +$300 per year, now makes sense as these expenses would pay down within a five-year period.

> NOTE:
> Always try and repair something instead of replacing it. Repairs
> can be expensed in full the year they are paid out. If you replace
> an appliance or land fixture, you need to capitalize your expense
> over its useful life. In the case of replacing a driveway, the capi-
> talization period is seventeen years!

I give this example so you can understand the thought processes you
must develop to be a successful investor. In short, before beginning any
renovation project you need to *carefully* evaluate all your options and
not lose site of the goal of staying in a positive cash flow.

Appliances: Used or New?

It used to be there was only one correct answer for this question: "Buy
used." With the advent of home improvement centers and overseas
manufacturing, costs for appliances have dropped dramatically in the
last several years. I typically buy my appliances new at the local home
improvement center. I buy the absolute cheapest brand they offer.
Today's new appliances cost about the same as good used appliances.
You can, however, consider buying used for washers, dryers, stoves, and
refrigerators. The used appliance dealers will claim that their used
Maytag will outlast your new cheap brand model. The verdict is still
out for me whether it makes more sense to buy used or new.
Dishwashers you must buy new. They are simply too cheap now, so
there is no market for buying them used.

Landscaping

Landscaping is very costly, especially in the southern and western
states, where the growing seasons are long. There are really no magic
bullets I can suggest here in order to curtail your costs in this area. My
only advice is not to buy any buildings that require extensive landscaping. If you do, make sure you can require the tenant to do the

work. Having the tenant do the landscaping, however, only works for single-family homes or multifamily units with defined yards for each tenant. If you need a landscaping service, my advice is to shop around until you find a good cheap service. Never agree to a monthly service, as these are costly. It may sound cheap when a landscaper tells you they can cut the grass for $25 until you find out the service cuts it every two weeks whether it needs it or not. In such a case you are actually paying $50 per month. One way to keep costs down in this area, although it requires more work for the owner, is simply to drive by your units frequently during the growing seasons. You can then just call in for lawn service when the grass needs cutting. You can also get your own lawn cut by the same service, then benchmark the frequency of the cuttings of your rental properties based upon your own lawn. We find this is a pretty dependable method and it tends to keep the landscaping costs down to a minimum.

Renting to Students

I cover the management of student property in a separate section as the issues are completely different from managing non-student properties. Because of this, if you end up using a management company, ensure that they have experience renting to students. If they do not have any prior experience, be sure they are willing to be educated and take on such properties.

Girls, Guys, One, Two, Three, or Four Bedrooms

Renting to students can be very profitable. It can also be very stressful, especially for the scrupulous landlord who has a fetish for order. Students are young, and for the most part, carefree—my apologies to the mature ones out there. The males—as we males know—are generally the worst offenders. I have a website for advertising student rentals where I post a survey that students fill out. I find this useful in keeping up with the current trends in student housing wants and needs. If you ask male students to rank their most important feature in a rental property (I actually did this), they quickly skip past the inanimate attributes such as privacy, available parking, or price, and go straight to women, and the availability thereof. The point is, as we know, at this age your number one goal is to party and score with the "chicks"—my apologies again for the hard-working guys out there. Women at this age are somewhat more mature, but parties and socializing still rank high on their list. What implications does this have for the owner of student rental properties? The women, although less prone to destroying your house with parties, are less proud than the males, and will tend to call about every little repair or bump in the driveway. This will cost you dearly in maintenance calls as compared to non-student rentals. The men, on the other hand, won't call at all about any repairs. They will walk through puddles in the kitchen for months from a leaking dishwasher and not call a single time to complain. Why? They are afraid they will get in trouble for the hole in the wall from their last party. Another issue with female students is that they tend not to get along as swimmingly as guys when grouped in numbers greater than two. These observations and others have thus led us to our ten rules of renting to students.

Ten Rules of Renting to Students

1. Male students will tend to "trash" a place more frequently than female students.

2. Apartments of greater than three bedrooms tend to be party magnets.

3. Single-family homes are party magnets for students (see 2 above).

4. Typically girls will tend to cost you a lot in service calls compared to guys.

5. You will have more roommate issues and turnover with girls than with guys.

6. Never rent a single-family home to guys (see 1 and 2) unless it is virtually indestructible.

7. As a rule, one- to two-bedroom living spaces are the best balance between income and keeping a lid on parties and trashing your units.

8. If you rent to four or more students in a single dwelling, be sure the unit, and more importantly the neighbors, will tolerate an occasional (or frequent) party.

9. Perform a walk-thorough at least quarterly in single-family homes that are at high risk for damage (three or more students).

10. Although profits are greatest for four or more students, risks are correspondingly higher as well.

Older units are therefore more suited for male students who will tend to call less frequently about minor repairs or inconveniences. These older units are also more indestructible and therefore more party-resistant. Single-family homes are best suited for women, especially for four-bedroom situations. We once had a four-bedroom house rented to four boys. We never had a single-service call over a one-year period. When we finally did see it (we failed to do our quarterly walk-through), the place was absolutely destroyed. They had actually built (using 2 x 4 framing) a full-sized Tiki bar in the living room. They had drilled holes in the ceilings to run stereo wires. They had sawed a hole in the floor of the closet to access the old basement where they brewed beer in large quantities. It required over $2,500 in repairs that we never fully received. The next set of guys we had were pretty much the same, except this time we intervened and had them pay for repairs upfront, before the lease expiration. The girls we had rented to, however, kept the place very nice. Although with the girls, we paid dearly in service calls and had constant roommate turnover and lease changes.

> NOTE:
> Although constant phone calls about little things like a bad light bulb or stuck window can be irritating and costly, when you receive no calls for repairs then it is time for you to perform a walk-through inspection.

Of course, you cannot discriminate between girls and guys, but you can be more prompt in responding to inquiries, if you get my drift. So in summary, the decision is yours as to where you want to fit in—I am only providing the guidelines. By understanding your customer you can better match your dwelling with student type and enjoy a more peaceful and profitable business.

Students and Leases

A big risk that you have with student rentals that doesn't exist with non-student rentals is that the timing of your leasing activities is absolutely crucial. If you fail to make the start of class the cutoff for students, you may find yourself sitting on a vacant unit until the semester ends six months or even an entire year later. For these reasons you must be pro-active, and ultimately successful, time and time again about getting your units rented in a very short time window. Never use anything less than a twelve-month lease and ensure that you use the proper lease expiry for students in your area. This is typically the end of the last month before classes begin in the fall. Occasionally you can fill a vacancy in the winter semester, but it is difficult. Have one lease per unit and have all students sign the lease so they are both individually and jointly responsible. Do not allow subletting. If you have an irreconcilable case of roommate trouble, allow a tenant to leave only after finding a suitable substitute, and then enter that new roommate on the lease. For the same reasons as discussed previously under rooming houses, do not allow individual leases for each student and bedroom. With students, individual leases are the worst, from the owner's perspective. The expiry dates on the leases will eventually not match, which means roommates will be coming and going and students will have little control over who their roommates are. This is especially problematic as they are no longer jointly responsible for the apartment. Who is to be held accountable for the carpet burn in the (common area) living room or the gouge in the kitchen vinyl floor? If the new roommate that no one knows has a habit of playing music at 2 a.m. you may have a full-blown mutiny on your hands. Worst yet, you might find everyone moves out but him. Also be sure and include a parental cosign form with your leases. This helps if there are damages that the students cannot (or will not) pay.

Finally, a word on pets and security deposits in student rentals. With or without pets, collect the maximum allowed security deposit for your state. Typically this is 1.5–2 times the monthly rent. This is just *better* insurance that you will have enough to cover any eventual damages you may find. If you do allow your students to have pets, please read the section on pets in this chapter to ensure you have the correct pet policies in place. We have found that students and pets typically do not work out well. Why? For a student away from home, a pet typically is not the family ten-year-old, thirty-pound terrier, but more likely a thirty-pound boxer puppy or a new kitten from the shelter around the corner. Student schedules and levels of maturity (once again, my apologies to the mature ones) can also lead to trouble. There are also potential roommate issues that crop up with a pet in the house where the owner is not taking care of it. Obviously these are not hard-fast rules. We once had a graduate student who had a dog for three years without incident. With students, however, these are the exceptions, not the rules.

Summary

- If you already have a day job that supports your real estate investing, you should hire a management company.

- Only use management companies that use tenant databases or otherwise have access to the credit bureaus.

- Do not accept a tenant application with no previous rental history.

- A tenant warning letter about a lease violation should always contain a consequence if the violation is not corrected and a *deadline*.

INSURANCE 12

As a landlord you will need insurance coverage in addition to what is common to a typical owner-occupied homeowners' insurance policy. At a minimum, rental property owners should carry the following types of insurance in order of importance:

1. Property and Casualty Insurance

2. General Liability Insurance

3. Loss of Rents Insurance

4. Umbrella Insurance

If you live in an earthquake or flood zone, then you would need to consider coverage for those items as well.

If you only own one or two rental properties, most homeowner policies will allow you to add your rental properties to your existing policy. There are usually limits as to the number of properties your primary carrier will allow. If you own several properties, or larger apartment buildings, you may need a commercial insurance policy. The thought is that if you have more than several rental properties, it is likely a business, and not related to your home activities. The typical homeowners' policy has two main sections: Section I covers your property, and Section II provides personal liability coverage (to cover you in case of lawsuits arising from things that happen on your property).

Property and Casualty Insurance

When getting quotes for your investment property you may find there are two types of insurance. The first type is what is called a basic *Fire Policy*. This policy only covers a standard set of perils and is sometimes referred to as a *dwelling property one*, or DP-1 policy. This policy typically covers you against the following eleven common perils:

1. fire or lightning

2. loss of property removed from premises because of fire or other perils

3. windstorm or hail

4. explosion

5. riots and other civil commotions

6. aircraft

7. vehicles

8. smoke

9. vandalism and malicious mischief

10. theft

11. breakage of glass that is part of the building

DP-1 policies are inexpensive and tempting to purchase but this is not what you want. You want the other "special" policy that provides additional coverage such as:

12. falling objects

13. weight of ice or snow

14. collapse of a building or any part thereof

15. sudden and accidental tearing apart, cracking, burning, or bulging of a steam or hot water heating system or of appliances for heating water

16. accidental discharge, leakage, or overflow of water or steam from within a plumbing, heating, or air-conditioning system or a domestic appliance

17. freezing of plumbing, heating, and air conditioning systems and domestic appliances

18. sudden and accidental injury from electrical currents generated by appliances, devices, fixtures, and wiring

19. loss of rent coverage due to any of the perils covered

These policies cover additional perils that are not covered under DP-1 policies, such as ice storms, injury, and water damages (except flooding). These policies are sometimes referred to as DP-3 policies. Note that this latter coverage has loss of rents coverage. For the investor, the loss of rent coverage is most important, so make sure you have it. This will ensure that you still receive rental income when your tenant burns your building down and he or she decides to move elsewhere. Your loss of rents coverage should be sufficient to cover six to twelve months. Make sure that the property dwelling coverage is sufficient to rebuild it back to original condition if it burns to the ground. Unlike your primary residence, where you can exceed the coverage amount by a certain percent if you go over budget in replacing your property, with rental properties you typically do not have this replacement insurance. With rental properties your building allowance is typically a fixed value that you cannot exceed. Either way, you need to ask your insurance agent and ensure that you have enough coverage to fully replace your structure. Find out the construction costs per square foot in your area and make sure the insurance company "calculators" come up with enough coverage for your property. I have had to adjust my coverage on several occasions because the values the insurance company proposed were too low. It only costs you an additional $25 per year to add another $20,000 on your dwelling, so it is worth it.

Policy Deductibles

Choosing high deductibles (as much as you can afford) is recommended. Your insurance should be reserved for the catastrophic events, and not be used to repair $1,000 damage. Another good reason to keep your deductibles high, and thus limit your use to larger damages, is that insurance companies are becoming increasingly more predatory with clients who have filed multiple claims. If you file even one claim it may affect your ability to have other properties insured (more on this later). Higher deductibles also are a good way to keep the premiums low, which adds to your bottom line.

Personal Property

Unlike with your primary residence, you do not need contents insurance for valuables that would be the responsibility of your tenants. You do, however, need to ensure you are covered for your *personal belongings* such as the stove, refrigerator, dishwasher, washer, dryer, etc., or whatever you own that is at risk in the dwelling.

General Liability Insurance

With the exception of a basic Fire Policy discussed earlier, most homeowner policies will offer some type of general liability and negligence coverage. Be sure, however, that personal injury is addressed in your policy. Specifically, the following personal injury areas are important for landlords:

- libel, slander, fraud, misrepresentation

- discrimination lawsuites

- allegations of fraud or misrepresentation

- malicious intent

Sometimes extra endorsements are required to obtain this additional personal injury coverage, so be sure to ask.

Typically, sufficient liability insurance can be acquired by purchasing an umbrella policy with your primary carrier or by insuring each separate property to a certain liability limit. The most common approach is using the umbrella policy. You would then simply list your rental properties under your umbrella policy. Be sure the individual properties in fact do get listed and ask for written proof of this. It is important that each property, whether insured by your primary carrier or not, have a liability limit that matches the lower limit of your umbrella policy. This is necessary so that you do not have a gap between your upper liability limit on your properties (and auto) and where your umbrella takes over. If you do have a gap, in the event of a claim you are liable to make up the difference before your umbrella kicks in. If you are unsure about this, ask your agent to clarify it. Regarding how much insurance is enough, I hesitate to weigh in on this question. I recommend instead that you talk to your insurance agent or an attorney. You obviously want to have enough coverage to protect your assets. We used to carry about $5,000,000 in general liability coverage, but we have recently lowered this to $2,000,000. Our rationale is that our equity is pretty evenly distributed among many properties and therefore is not an easy target for a liability claim. Look at things from the plaintiff's angle. This amount of money would most likely satisfy any type of lawsuit you may face. It would be unlikely anyone would seek to exceed this limit and go after your personal assets to extract an extra sum of money. The bottom line is that each case needs to be evaluated separately. At the risk of generalizing, for most folks with personal assets of less than $1,000,000, $2,000,000–$5,000,000 of coverage is probably more than sufficient.

Business Owners Package

As you accumulate more properties or purchase larger apartment buildings it becomes increasingly difficult to have your properties insured through your primary insurance carrier. In such cases you have several options. When you reach your allowed limit of rental properties through your primary carrier, you can simply add other properties ad-hoc through other carriers. The other way to obtain coverage is by purchasing a *Business Owners Package* that bundles all available coverage into one policy. Included in a Business Owners Package would be fire coverage (written on a special form basis), loss of rents, theft of money, or loss of business property owned by the insured.

> NOTE:
> Most insurance companies will not write a Business Owners Package on a rental dwelling of less than four units.

Business Owners Packages are usually competitively priced; however, the underwriting is more conservative and the product is only offered for good quality buildings. Typical exclusions to this type of policy include employment practices liability, wrongful termination, sexual harassment, discrimination, and earthquake coverage. You can typically buy additional insurance to cover your risk in these areas.

Reducing the Risks of Lawsuits

In addition to maintaining adequate property, casualty, and general liability insurance, there are several management practices that can help reduce the chance that a tenant will sue you.

Don't Befriend Your Tenants

The best way to avoid confrontation is to avoid confrontation. A land-lord should always be polite and courteous to a tenant, but not neces-sarily friendly. Don't engage in small talk or discuss your personal life. The less attention you draw to yourself and your rental property busi-ness, the less likely your tenant is going to sue you.

Don't Allow Dogs, or If You Do, Limit the Weight

We assume you will use good judgment and not rent to tenants who have snakes, crocodiles, or lions, and will therefore limit our discus-sion to dogs. A docile dog, like a labrador retriever, obviously poses little liability risk. A pit bull on the other hand is a different story. Insurance companies are aware of these risks and most companies have a list of dogs that are *not* covered under their policy. If you do allow dogs, be sure you obtain this list so you are aware of which breeds to avoid. Be alert to the fact that the list is not restricted to pure breeds, but extends to mixed breeds as well. Thus, if the dog in question is part labrador retriever and part pit bull, you may still be held liable in a negligence case. I have asked my insurance agent specifically about this mixed breed issue. I was told that only a veteri-narian could prove or disprove the presence of a particular breed in a dog. If you do decide to allow dogs, my recommendation would be to restrict the weight limit to twenty-five pounds.

Form a Separate Business Entity for Your Rental Property

In order to limit liability exposure many landlords transfer the title of their rental property to a separate business entity, such as a limited liability corporation (LLC), Subchapter S corporation, or family trust. This way your personal assets and business assets are separated. The idea is that in most cases, any liability claim incurred by the business entity would be limited to the business entities assets. Attorneys have told me, however, that such *corporate shields* are still vulnerable. Additionally, for tax purposes, such businesses must be treated separately from your individual tax return, and in some cases taxes must be filed quarterly. Whether or not this approach makes sense for you should be determined by consulting with an attorney.

Use a Professional Management Company

By using a professional management company you will likely reduce your risk of being sued. Management companies are usually real estate professionals and thus understand the legal aspects of renting real estate. Your inclination may be to throw the tenant and all his or her belongings out on the street when his or her rent is late. Management companies know better and will follow the law and keep landlords out of trouble. Since they are also potentially at risk, they are quick to point out potential opportunities for a lawsuit.

Mold

Lawsuits seeking recovery for personal injuries and property damages resulting from mold have become increasingly more common and thus deserve special comment. Typical health problems associated with mold exposure are respiratory ailments that include runny nose, cough, congestion, and aggravation of asthma. Over the past few years, many insurers have reduced or eliminated mold coverage from property liability policies. Typically mold will be covered if it results from a covered peril. If there is no identifiable source, or the mold cannot be traced to a covered peril, the owner is liable. Property owners should determine whether existing property or liability insurance policies cover property damage, personal injury, and business interruption claims resulting from mold. Mold testing kits are now available to the public for a few dollars, posing an even greater liability risk to landlords if tenants suspect the presence of mold. With the absence of available insurance coverage, landlords must resort to preventative measures to avoid being exposed to this liability. As long as moisture is present, mold can reproduce. To stop mold, the source of water must be eliminated. Common sources of mold-forming moisture could be a leaking roof, exterior wall leaks, condensation, foundation leaks, and improperly sized air conditioners that do not effectively dehumidify. Any cellulose-containing material coupled with an ambient temperature is ideal for mold growth. Mold can begin forming within forty-eight hours, so if you have a roof leak, move quickly to repair it. Also be sure to keep good records on your response to such leaks. Preventative measures to avoid mold such as yearly roof/property inspections may also be advisable. As a final note, if you incur water damage, carefully consider whether you should file an insurance claim. Claims are reported to the *Comprehensive Loss Underwriting Exchange* (CLUE) and thus become public knowledge. When you go to sell the property the buyer may not be able to obtain insurance, as his prospective carrier will likely see the CLUE report and suspect possible mold damage.

Claims Histories and the CLUE Report

It is a good practice to limit use of your insurance to catastrophic events. The reason is that insurance companies are becoming more and more reluctant to insure customers who have previous claims histories. All claims, whether on your primary residence or investment property, get reported to what is known as the *Comprehensive Loss Underwriting Exchange*, more commonly referred to as the CLUE. CLUE reports are similar in nature to credit bureau reports. We had a situation once where a tree had fallen from our side of the property line onto our neighbor's side of the property line. We found out because we received a letter describing how a tree had damaged their garage and we should therefore pay for the damages. We were cited to be liable because the tree was dead, and therefore our responsibility. I went by and personally inspected the property and saw that no damage was done to their garage or anything else, so I naturally refused any payment. The neighbor then contacted her insurance company and filed a liability claim against me. I contacted my insurance company and they sent out a claims investigator per standard procedures. The claims investigator completed her investigation and eventually wrote a letter denying the claim and exonerating me from any liability. Her conclusion was that I had no way of knowing that such a peril threatened the neighbor's property as it was out of my view. Had the neighbor written me beforehand, and put me on notice about this tree, I would have then been liable. Feeling victorious, I was glad to put this rather irritating event behind me, or so I thought. It was two years later and I had long since forgotten about this event until I was shopping to find a cheaper source of insurance. Suddenly I was getting the cold shoulder from all the big carriers. Since my credit scores are high, I was confused. Eventually I discovered that no carriers would approve me because of this single liability claim against one of my properties. For the record, I had absolutely no prior claims, so in fact I was actually a model customer. Not so, according to the CLUE report. The companies that rejected me informed me that a liability claim was listed on my CLUE report. Even though it was a zero payout, it precluded them from insuring me. I eventually found a carrier that would take me based on more rational selection methods, but I spent the better part of a week on the phone looking for a carrier. The upshot is as follows: as a landlord, you can't avoid such occurrences. These are simply part of playing the game and being an owner of investment property. What you can do, though, is be aware of the potential damage such an innocuous situation can cause. Similar to credit reports that persist for seven years, CLUE reports are on record for five years. Also noteworthy is that if you have two claims within five years on the same house, you will have great difficulty changing or obtaining new insurance for *any* property. Interestingly enough, it doesn't matter whether you filed the claims on record yourself or the previous owner filed them as the following example will illustrate. We recently purchased a new house to live in and the previous owner had filed two claims within the last five years (one for hurricane damage and one for fire damage) for a total of $8,000 for the two claims. After at least ten companies had refused to carry us because of this, we eventually were able to obtain coverage. I wish I could list the companies that rejected us, but suffice to say, you are probably insured with one of them! Similar to the consumer protection changes regarding credit reporting laws, I am sure these CLUE reports will get increasingly more attention from the government. As more injustices present themselves they will increasingly find their way into our court systems, culminating in better consumer protection laws. Until then, I suggest playing the defensive role and *do not* use your insurance unless you need to. Additionally, be sure you quickly address any liability challenges and try to resolve them without involving your insurance agent.

Summary

- The following types of insurance are recommend for landlords: Property and Casualty Insurance, General Liability Insurance, Loss of Rents Insurance, and Umbrella Insurance.

- It is a good practice to limit the use of your insurance to catastrophic events to avoid being reported to the Comprehensive Loss Underwriting Exchange (CLUE).

- Choose higher deductibles to keep the premium low and cash flow as high as possible.

- Lawsuits resulting from mold have become more common and it is important for landlords to pay attention to any conditions that might support the growth of mold.

- Forming a limited liability corporation (LLC), Subchapter S corporation, or family trust for your properties may protect your personal assets, but such corporate shields are still vulnerable.

TAXES AND RENTAL PROPERTY

Whether you decide to use an accountant or not, you need to understand the basic tax laws as they apply to rental property owners. These tax laws will govern your decisions on managing, upgrading, performing repairs or major renovations, and ultimately, selling your properties. The purpose of the following discussion is to provide you with enough information so that you are able to prepare your taxes with the help of tax preparation software. For those readers who have very complicated returns, or have the need to squeeze out that extra dollar, you are encouraged to seek out a good accountant. The IRS website also offers an excellent resource for the interested reader. We will start by presenting a general overview, and then proceed to go into more detail on areas that are most important to real estate investors.

Historical Overview

Prior to 1986, a taxpayer could generally deduct real estate losses in full from ordinary (non-real estate) income. For example, if you owned rental property, and at the end of the year your net real estate loss totaled $30,000, you could deduct that amount in full from your taxable income. These tax write-offs gave rise to significant numbers of investors who invested in real estate just to shelter their taxes. In response to this growing tax shelter industry, the Reagan Administration enacted *The Tax Reform Act of 1986*, which added Internal Revenue Code section 469 (IRC §469). This tax code limited the taxpayer's ability to deduct real estate losses from ordinary wage income by introducing new concepts, such as *passive activity* and *passive activity loss rules*. The result was that real estate losses could only be used to off set real estate gains, thus limiting the taxpayer's ability to write off losses against ordinary (non-passive) income. There are, however, important exceptions to the passive activity loss rules. Each taxpayer is allowed to use $25,000 in real estate losses to off set non-passive (ordinary) income with certain salary phase-out rules. Also, provisions were made so that taxpayers could carry forward any disallowed losses until they sold their rental property. Although at times complex, understanding how these rules affect the owners of rental property is important.

Passive and Non-Passive Income and Losses

In general, unless you are a real estate professional, all rental activities are considered passive activities. All remaining sources of income or losses are considered non-passive. Making a distinction between passive and non-passive activities is important. This is because you can deduct a passive loss only against income generated from a passive gain. Since real estate is defined as a passive activity, the result is that (generally) you can only use real estate losses to offset real estate gains. As an example, if you had $10,000 in rental income and $15,000 in expenses, your loss would be limited to your gain of $10,000. You could not use this $5,000 of your rental property losses to offset your ordinary income. Fortunately, for most of us, there is an exclusion to this rule. The IRS has a $25,000 special allowance rule. If you or your spouse actively participated in a rental real estate activity, you can deduct up to $25,000 of loss from the rental activity from your ordinary income.

NOTE:
These definitions are not necessarily logical. For example "passive-like" activities, such as stock investing, are considered to be non-passive activities.

The $25,000 Exclusion Rule

Rental real estate losses up to $25,000 may be deducted from your non-passive (ordinary) wages by an individual who actively participates. If you own more than a 10% interest, and you make any management decisions, you will qualify as an active participant. Nearly all landlords will be able to check this box come tax time. The $25,000 special allowance is reduced if your modified adjusted gross income (MAGI) exceeds $100,000 and is phased out at a rate of fifty cents for every dollar over $100,000. Therefore, when your MAGI exceeds $150,000, the deduction is completely phased out. MAGI is essentially your adjusted gross income (AGI) with some minor modifications. As an example of how this phase-out rule works, if your MAGI is $125,000, you are only allowed to deduct $12,500 in real estate losses that year. If you fall within this income category, and especially if you are borderline, be sure you are maximizing your 401(K), IRA, etc., or any vehicles that may bring your MAGI below this $100,000 level. I recommend talking to an accountant who can probably suggest other creative solutions. If your rental business is large, and occupies most of your time, one way you can avoid having a limit on your allowable losses is to become a real estate professional. Real estate professionals are not limited to this $25,000 exclusion and can deduct any amount of rental property losses regardless of MAGI. Be aware, though, that to qualify as a real estate professional, you must pass more stringent tests than the "active participation" condition. One of the requirements is that you must be a *material participant* in your business. Material participation is often confused with active participation but is actually quite different. While it is easy to qualify as an active participant, and thus be eligible for the $25,000 exclusion, qualifying as a material participant is much more difficult. The IRS has specific rules about how much time you must spend on your real estate business per week to qualify. In general, if real estate is not your primary source of income, it is difficult to pass the *material participation test*. Once again, please talk to an accountant if you are unsure. For most of us, then, the $25,000 exclusion applies, and thus our deductions are limited to this amount.

> NOTE:
> The definition of *active participation* has nothing to do with passive and non-passive activities. The passive and non-passive activities are used to categorize types of incomes and losses. *Active participation* defines your level of involvement in your real estate activities.

If your real estate losses in any one year exceed the $25,000, or you are limited by the salary phase-out rule, you do not lose these deductions. These deductions carry forward until you reach a year when you are eligible to use those deductions. Another means you have to use up your suspended losses is to sell a rental property. In the year of the sale, regardless of your income or circumstance, you can deduct all previously disallowed real estate losses up to the limit of your gain. This makes sense, since all real estate activities are passive activities and thus real estate losses can be used to offset real estate (passive) gains. The following examples illustrate the application of these tax rules:

Year 1: John and Mary have a MAGI of $94,000 and a net rental loss for the year of $25,000. They actively participated in the rental activity and their MAGI is less than $100,000, so they qualify for the full $25,000 exclusion. They may offset their ordinary income with this $25,000 and thus lower their taxable income.

Year 2: John and Mary have a MAGI of $110,000 and a rental loss for the year of $25,000. Their MAGI is greater than $100,000, so the phase-out rule applies and their allowable deduction is reduced to $20,000. Since their losses exceeded their allowable deduction, they can only deduct $20,000 and they carry forward the disallowed $5,000.

Year 5: John and Mary now have had a MAGI of over $150,000 for years 3 and 4, so they are not eligible for any deductions. During this period they have accumulated disallowed losses totaling $40,000. They sell one of their rental properties and end up with a taxable gain of $70,000. Their losses that year on their other rental properties are $20,000. Normally their MAGI would prevent them from any deductions, but since they have a gain this year of $70,000 in passive income, they can deduct all previous disallowed losses ($40,000) along with the current year's losses of $20,000. They need only to pay taxes on $10,000 of their gain from the sale of their rental property.

This $25,000 exclusion is most important in the early years of owning rental property. Even if you have a positive cash flow, you will usually end up with a net loss for the year. One reason for this is that rental property owners benefit from a deduction known as *depreciation*.

Depreciation

Depreciation is a deduction the IRS allows you to take on the land improvements of your rental property. Only the portion of a property's value that is attributable to the building(s), and not the land, can be depreciated. Residential rental property can be depreciated by either using a straight-line method over 27.5 years, or by using an accelerated schedule. In the year that you buy the rental property you must choose the type of depreciation you wish to use, and you also must assign a value to the depreciable portion of your property. Once you select a method of depreciation and assign your building value, it is fixed and generally cannot be changed. Determining the value of your building can be done in a number of ways. The simplest and safest method is just to look up the cost of the land from the tax records and subtract the land value from the sale price. Using this method of calculation, the depreciable portion on a duplex with a $170,000 sale price and a land (tax) value of $40,000 would be $130,000. To keep the math simple, let's assume we chose the straight line of depreciation. The depreciation of this building over 27.5 years would then result in an allowance of $4,727 per year. Depreciation is the only true tax deduction for rental property owners, as you get this deduction and incur no out-of-pocket expenses. In essence, depreciation is a non-economic *paper deduction*. It's also a big one. In this case, for example, even if your duplex broke even after expenses and income, you would still be able to deduct the depreciation portion from your ordinary income.

By now the question in everyone's mind is likely, "How can I maximize this paper loss deduction?" One way to maximize your depreciation is to allocate less value to the land and more value to the building. In fact, the IRS has no requirement on the method you use to allocate value, thus *how* you divide the cost between the land and the building is somewhat subjective, so long as you can justify how you arrived at your number.[14] Before you go off in search of the best method to maximize your free depreciation tax break, hold on a minute. If depreciation seems too good to be true, you are partly correct. With few exceptions, the IRS will see to it that you pay back (at some point) every penny of the depreciation tax deductions you enjoyed over the years. For example, if you sell your building and are not doing a 1031 tax exchange (more on this later) then you must pay back the depreciation you took over the years. Using the current duplex example, with a depreciation of $4,727 per year, if you owned the property five years, you would need to pay taxes on any gain from the sale *plus* $21,135 ($4,727 x 5) in depreciation you took over the years. The sale of a rental property you have owned and depreciated for many years can thus be very costly without applying some other type of tax shelter. Knowing this fact, you may consider not taking any depreciation at all. After all, if you don't take this depreciation then you don't need to pay taxes on it when you sell, right? Once again, the IRS has thought this through a bit more than you or me. If you did not take any depreciation, then when you sell that property, the IRS will require you to go back and calculate things *as if* you had taken it. You then have the misfortune to pay taxes on a sum you never deducted in the first place! Although this *depreciation recapture* is an unpleasant side effect of the tax benefit, depreciation is still a very good deal. Since you are required to take the depreciation by the IRS, the best approach is just to take the fair depreciation based upon tax records, and enjoy your tax benefit.

NOTE:
You don't need to tell the IRS how you determine your allocation to land but you should have a record of it in case you are asked. There have been cases where the IRS has challenged property owners who have submitted abnormally low allocations to the land. Obviously, the safest approach is to use tax record values of the land.

Repairs and Improvements

The IRS differentiates between a repair and an improvement. You can expense (deduct) the cost of repairs in full in the year you made them. You cannot deduct the cost of improvements. You recover the cost of improvements by taking depreciation. Personal property, such as free standing appliances, also must be depreciated. Because of the distinction between a repair and an improvement, it is important to understand how to categorize these expenses come tax time. The IRS provides the following definitions for repairs and improvements.

"A repair keeps your property in good operating condition. It does not materially add to the value of your property or substantially prolong its life. Repainting your property inside or out, fixing gutters or floors, fixing leaks, plastering, and replacing broken windows are examples of repairs. If you

make repairs as part of an extensive remodeling or restoration of your property, the whole job is an improvement.

"An improvement adds to the value of property, prolongs its useful life, or adapts it to new uses. If you make an improvement to property, the cost of the improvement must be capitalized. The capitalized cost can generally be depreciated as if the improvement were separate property."

Examples of improvements are a new roof, furnace, deck, driveway, or a fence. A new roof or furnace is considered part of the original structure and is depreciated over 27.5 years, if you chose the straight-line method of depreciation. A fence is depreciated over fifteen years. Unattached personal property, such as freestanding appliances, are depreciated over five years, and may not be expensed in the year they were purchased. New carpets, likewise, are treated as an improvement expensed over five years. For most common items, there are depreciation schedules that you can access online at the IRS website.

Whether you expense something (as a repair) and thus claim the deduction in full in the year it was expensed, or whether you need to capitalize it (depreciate it) over its usable life can be a very gray area. For example, a fully rebuilt furnace may qualify as a repair and be expensed in full in the year of the repair. A furnace that was replaced, however, must be depreciated. In general, the IRS states that if the expenditure served to "materially add to the value of the property, or prolong its active life," it is a capital improvement expense. If you are uncertain whether something is a repair or a capital expense, you should go to the IRS website and research it, or consult an accountant. In a recent case, a landlord was successful in claiming an $8,000 roof repair as an expense, and not a capital expense, that would typically need to be depreciated. Since this case is particularly instructive, I have summarized the court's findings below:

The court held that (the landlord) is entitled to deduct the entire $8,000 as a repair expense. The conclusions are reported verbatim below:

There was no replacement or substitution of the roof. The landlord's only purpose in having the work done to the roof was to prevent the leakage and keep her rental house in operating condition and not to prolong the life of the property, increase its value, or make it adaptable to another use. The landlord's expenditure merely restored her rental house to one with a roof free of leaks.

The IRS then summarized, *"it is necessary to take into consideration the purpose for which an expenditure is made in order to determine whether such expenditure is capital in nature or constitutes a current expense."*

Whether you expense something or capitalize it, you should be mindful of the gravity of the decision, especially for large expenses, like an $8,000 roof that may attract more scrutiny by the IRS. Whether you want to reside on the more aggressive or more conservative side of this fence is a question for you and/or your tax accountant.

Other Expenses

In addition to depreciation and the cost of repairs, you can deduct the following expenses from your rental income. All these items may be expensed in full in the year you paid for them:

- advertising

- cleaning and maintenance

- utilities

- insurance

- taxes

- interest

- points

- commissions

- tax return preparation fees

- travel expenses

- rental payments

- local transportation expenses

In short, you can expense just about anything that you paid for out of your pocket that is related to your rental property activity. Now that we are familiar with the basic deductions and expenses available to the owner of rental property, let's put it all together in an example. As you may already be aware, all your rental property income and expense activities are recorded on your Schedule E tax form. The IRS, though, has a particular way it likes to group expenses and income so it is instructive if we look at an example of a typical Schedule E tax form.

Schedule E

In the United States, all your rental property expenses and income are documented using a Schedule E tax form. Thus all your repairs, capital expenses (improvements), yearly depreciation allowance for your building, mortgage interest, insurance, property taxes, and appliances are captured on this one form. After all the expenses are compared to the income, you have a single number at the bottom. This number is either positive or negative, depending on how you did that year. This number is then carried over to the front page of your taxes. If it is a positive number it will add to your gross income, and you will pay more taxes. If it is a negative number, it will subtract from your income, according to the $25,000 special allowance rules, and you will pay less taxes. Typically, due largely to the "paper loss" deduction from depreciation, new owners will enjoy a net tax advantage, meaning that the number you carry over will be a negative number. Let's look at a typical example of a completed Schedule E tax form using our duplex example.

Typical Schedule E tax form for a duplex	
1. Rents and royalties:	$16,800
2. Advertising:	$100
3. Auto and travel:	$150
4. Cleaning and maintenance:	$1,000
5. Commissions:	N/A
6. Insurance:	$550
7. Legal and professions:	N/A
8. Management fees:	$840
9. Mortgage interest:	$7,397
10. Other interest:	N/A
11. Repairs:	$1000
12. Supplies:	$500

13. Taxes:	$1,400
14. Other:	N/A
Total Expenses:	($12,937)
Carry-forward Depreciations:	($250)*
Building Depreciation:	($ 4,727)
Total Expenses:	($17,914)
Total Income:	$16,800
Net rental loss or gain:	($1,114)

*This is your yearly depreciated capital expenses or personal property, such as appliances, new carpet, etc.

In this case, your tax deduction is $1,114. Note that without the building depreciation of $4,727 you would have realized a net gain and would be paying taxes on an additional $3,613. If you are in the 28% tax bracket, that would be an extra $1,000 out of your pocket. For this reason, unless your new rental property is a cash cow, your early investing years will usually produce a net tax advantage at year's end.

Lose the Paper and Calculator

In this final section we will discuss the advantages of using an automated tax program. Whether you decide to use an accountant or not, using these tax programs greatly simplifies your taxes. I know for certain that without the help of these tax programs I could never prepare my own taxes. We have been using tax preparation software for the past eight years. Our taxes last year were over one hundred pages. I had sold rental properties and bought rental properties. I had over $36,000 in suspended passive income that the software automatically accounted for and carried over. It remembers my depreciation schedule from properties I bought eight years ago, and keeps track of the washers and dryers I depreciate over a five-year schedule, carrying forward the correct dollar amount every year. All I have to do each year is import the previous year's data and answer the basic interview questions, like, "Did I buy a new rental property? What date did I buy it?" The software then calculates the depreciation schedule automatically and shows you the number. Did you have any repairs? How much were those repairs? Well, you get the idea. The only, and I repeat only, calculation I have had to make on my own is the actual adjusted basis I had in the property I sold. The last two years the tax program actually calculates the complicated alternative minimum tax. I actually learned everything I know about passive income loss limitations by studying my taxes *after* I got the final answer, so to speak. In short, it is really quite an extraordinary feat that these tax programs accomplish every year. Most of these tax program services also offer accountants who will review your tax return for a small fee. These tax programs thus offer a great way to do-it-yourself and avoid the extra costs of hiring an accountant. It also necessitates that you understand (just) enough about tax law to appreciate the consequences of your tax decisions. Please understand that I am not suggesting these programs can replace a good creative accountant. I am only making the point that such tax programs are easy to use and in many cases provide a similar result to what you would obtain from an accountant. Additionally, one could argue that since these programs are derived from tested algorisms, the calculations will normally be correct. As long as you answer the questions truthfully and provide accurate information, taxes submitted with these programs should be less prone to audits by the IRS.

Summary

- Prior to 1986, a taxpayer could generally deduct real estate losses in full from ordinary (non–real estate) income.

- The Tax Reform Act of 1986 introduced the "passive activity loss rules," which provided that real estate losses could only be used to offset real estate gains, thus limiting the taxpayer's ability to write off losses against ordinary (non-passive) income.

- An important exception to the "passive activity loss rules" that each taxpayer is allowed to use $25,000 in real estate losses to offset non-passive (ordinary) income.

- The $25,000 special allowance is reduced if your modified adjusted gross income (MAGI) exceeds $100,000 and is phased out completely when your MAGI reaches $150,000.

- Depreciation is a deduction the IRS allows you to take on the land improvements of your rental property.

- A repair keeps your property in good operating condition and does not materially add to the value of your property or substantially prolong its life.

- An improvement adds to the value of property, prolongs its useful life, or adapts it to new uses.

- Repairs can be expensed in the year they were performed, but improvements must be depreciated over their effective useful life as if the improvements were separate property.

SELLING YOUR PROPERTY

14

A number of years ago my wife and I owned five properties, three of which were single-family homes. At the time we bought them we told ourselves we would never sell, but instead we would pay these properties off and own them free and clear twenty years hence. In just five short years, though, we ended up selling all three of our single-family dwellings, and replacing them with multifamily properties. In this case, we sold in response to a local downturn in the single-family market. The take-home message is that regardless of their long-term plans, landlords need to understand the fundamentals of selling their properties, both from tax standpoint as well as from a "how to" perspective.

Preparing for the Sale

In preparing for a sale, the first thing on your agenda is getting your property ready to market. This process can be divided into two categories: properties that will be sold as investment properties, and properties that will be sold as owner-occupied. Most multifamily dwellings will fall under the investment grade category, but single-family homes, condominiums, and townhomes can be marketed as either investment or owner-occupied properties. The level of preparation and focus of your efforts will be different in both cases. Buyers who are investors will want to see the property leased up and commanding a good rent.

Alternatively, a buyer who will live in the property will be more interested in appearances than income potential.

Selling as Owner-Occupied Dwellings

If you plan on targeting the owner-occupied housing market, much work may be required to command full market value for your property. Rental property takes on a very distinctive look (think worn) after just a few years of use by tenants. The first step in preparing your property is to get rid of the tenants sometime between January and March. This will give you enough time to get in there and prepare the house for a spring sale. Your goal here is to make the property look like it has never been rented. I have used the following recipe many times and have always gotten the highest market value, and sold quickly, both with and without realtors. The quick sale is important. Remember, the house you are selling is not producing income, so making mortgage payments and paying utility bills for even several months can cut deeply into your profits. Begin by painting the outside of the house, if necessary, with a fresh bright color. Pay for landscaping, or do it yourself, so the curb appeal looks neat and clean. The same goes for the inside. If the house is very dated, you can do what I call a partial rehab. For the baths, replace vanity tops, fixtures, and flooring. Leave the old tubs or showers but resurface them (these products now exist at home improvement stores). Put up a new shower curtain—this helps take the eye away from any imperfections left behind. Paint the bathrooms as well. For the kitchen, replace worn countertops and flooring. If the kitchen cabinets are old, remove the hardware, repaint the cabinets, and put on new hardware. Paint the inside of the house, not white, but rather a cream color, and make sure the wall and ceiling preparations are done right so the job also looks neat and clean. Replace old-looking carpet with new. Wood floors should be treated with oil or some other finish that brings the shine back. Do not refinish them. This is too costly and you won't get any of that money back from the sale price. This whole partial rehab should cost no more than several thousand dollars. No worries, though—you will get this money back and more when you sell. As an added bonus, these expenses can be charged against the capital gain, thus reducing your taxes. We have used this technique repeatedly over many years with great success. This method has also been validated on two occasions where we had homes listed that sat vacant for many months. Performing these improvements led to a sale within days, often at a higher price than we had originally listed the house. Remember, your potential buyers of these homes are likely folks who have no experience, or more importantly, no interest in renovating a house themselves. Let's face it—unless there is something extraordinary about your house, prospective buyers will simply move on to the next house that is more appealing. Your average homebuyer does not have the imagination or the fortitude to buy an unfinished product. We live in a "now" society, and homes that need work typically do not sell quickly or at market price.

If you are selling an older home, it is a good idea to purchase a home warranty that you can offer with the sale. The warranty will typically cover repairs or replacements for one full year on mechanical systems and major built-in appliances that break down due to normal wear and tear. These warranties offer valuable protection on home heating, plumbing, electrical, central air conditioning systems, and many built-in appliances, and thus provide the buyer with added security. The several hundred dollars that these policies cost will go far in calming nervous first-time buyers.

Selling as Investment Properties

It doesn't matter whether you are selling a single-family home or a multiunit apartment building; if you plan on selling your property to an investor, a whole different set of criteria applies. For investment properties, it is not that critical how the inside appears. Of course, you don't want gaping holes in the ceilings or floors, but that aside, the inside should look neat and clean. The outside of the property should have a curb appeal comparable to other units in the neighborhood. If painting or landscaping is required to achieve this look, then you should do it. The biggest factor in selling an investment property will be making sure all the units are occupied, and commanding the highest possible rents. The arguments in favor of listing your investment property with tenants in place are many.

- Occupied properties produce income while they are on the market and thus remove the pressure from the seller to get a quick sale.

- Occupied properties hide imperfections and hinder close inspections.

- Occupied properties are typically worth more money to an investor than vacant properties.

- Vacant properties are susceptible to vandalism.

- Vacant properties may not be covered by your insurance policy after a certain period of vacancy.

Although keeping the tenants is beneficial to the owner, realtors prefer to list vacant properties, as they are easier to show. They also do not like to deal with the tenants, who are usually uncooperative. These problems, however, can be readily overcome. Here is what I have found to be a solution. For the inconvenience to your tenants, add an addendum to the lease agreement whereby the tenant is given a 20% discount on his or her rent. They are to pay their usual rent on time, however, 20% of the rent amount is placed into his or her deposit account each month. They will receive this 20% monthly bonus only after the close of escrow. A 20% discount is an aggressive discount and finds favor with most tenants. Inform the tenants that this discount is only valid if the property is made available for showings within reasonable hours and kept clean at all times. Although this approach requires a bit more work, it will lower your risk and net you a much greater profit than selling a vacant property.

Pricing, FSBOs, and Realtors

By now, you should have the skills to estimate the market value of your rental property yourself. If not, follow the valuation guidelines presented in Chapter 7. In addition, whether you plan on working with a realtor or not, you can always have one come by and estimate the value of your property. Using all these tools together, you should easily come up with a fair market value for your property. Obviously, if you are not in a rush to sell, and the rents are coming in, you can start by asking the higher-end price.

If you feel you can sell your property by owner, you should do so. You stand to gain about 5% more from the sale, which can be significant, especially on larger sales. The real question then is, do you *need* a realtor? There are several considerations as to whether you require a realtor or not. If your property has poor visibility and is buried three streets deep in a neighborhood, I would suggest using a realtor. If it is located on a four-lane thoroughfare, I would at least begin the advertising process by posting my own "for sale" sign out front. There are other situations where you may want to employ a Realtor. If you need to sell the property quickly, then you should hire a Realtor. If you are out-of-state or do not have the time, ability, or inclination to show your property, you should hire a Realtor. If you do use a Realtor, remember the rule of keeping any information that may be valuable to a buyer to yourself. For example, never divulge what your absolute bottom dollar would be. Although your Realtor may work for you, first and foremost, his or her goal is to sell the property as quickly as possible, so be discrete. Also, be sure to negotiate the sales commission. Be careful, though, when you negotiate down the Realtor's commission. Ensure the buyer's agents will still get the usual and customary fees for your area. Ask for a copy of the multiple listing and make sure that the usual rate goes to the buyer's agent (in our state this is 2.4%). If the percent commission paid to the buyer's agent is low, buyer's agents will overlook your property and take their buyers elsewhere where the commissions are higher. As an additional incentive to buyer's agents, in down markets, you can offer a $1,000 bonus to the buyer's agent who sells your property. This has the effect of increasing showings dramatically.

Alternatively, if you need the MLS exposure and don't necessarily require the aid of a real estate agent, you can shop around for a *flat fee MLS* service. The term *flat fee MLS* is used to describe the service and fee structure provided by real estate agents who offer real estate services on a limited service basis rather than as part of a bundled suite of services common to the traditional full-service model. Essentially it is not unlike a *For Sale By Owner* (FSBO), with the important exception that you have exposure to the MLS and other buyer's agents. Typically, with flat fee MLSs the fee is paid upfront when the property is listed rather than at settlement or closing, as is the case with traditional brokerage services.

Depreciation Recapture

As noted in Chapter 14, your depreciation deduction is a great tax break for owners of rental property; however, when you sell, the IRS demands that you pay taxes on all the depreciation you have taken on the property. The rate you pay on this amount depends on whether it is a long-term capital gain or a short-term gain. The short-term gains are taxed as ordinary income, whereas the long-term gains are taxed at a lower rate. As we noted earlier, you *must* take this depreciation whether you want to or not. If you don't take it, the IRS will demand that you *retrospectively* calculate how much depreciation you *should have* taken, and then it will make you pay taxes on that amount. The depreciation recapture is quite significant and can greatly add to your taxable gain, especially if you owned your property for many years.

Determining Your Taxable Gain

Selling an investment property is different than selling your main home. Different rules apply for calculating your taxes. Just like calculating capital gains, the formula for calculating the gain or loss of rental property involves subtracting your cost basis from your selling price. Anything that increases your basis lowers your taxable gain. Decreases to your basis, like depreciation recapture, increase your tax gains. The general formula used to determine your tax gain or loss when you sell your property is:

$$
\begin{aligned}
& \textit{Sale Price} \\
& - \textit{Adjusted Basis} \\
& \underline{+ \textit{Selling Expenses}} \\
& \textit{Tax Gain or Loss}
\end{aligned}
$$

The sale price is simply the price you sold your property for. The selling expenses would be commissions you paid to Realtors. Determining the adjusted cost basis is a bit more tedious. To determine the adjusted basis you would complete the following calculations:

$$
\begin{aligned}
& \textit{Basis (cost of the building)} \\
& + \textit{Capital Expenses (total of all capital improvements)} \\
& \underline{- \textit{Depreciation (accumulated building depreciation)}} \\
& \textit{Adjusted Basis}
\end{aligned}
$$

Profits on rental property can be taxed partly as ordinary gain and partly as capital gain. The depreciation recapture portion is taxed as ordinary income (because that is how you originally claimed it). The capital gains are taxed as either short term or long term depending on how long you owned the property. Ordinary gains are reported on Form 4797, and capital gains are reported on Schedule D. The following is an example calculation.

EXAMPLE:

John bought a duplex for $180,000 and owned it for exactly five years. In his first year of ownership John assigned a value of $100,000 for the building and $80,000 for the land portion using tax records. He chose the straight-line method of depreciation (27.5 years) and depreciated $3,636 each year for a total of $18,180 (5 x $3,636). He spent $10,000 on capital improvements for a new roof. John sold his property for $200,000 and paid $10,000 in sales commissions at closing.

His tax is calculated as follows:

Tax Gain Calculation:

Sale price:	$200,000	$200,000
Adjusted basis:		
Cost of building	$180,000	
Plus: Improvements	+ $10,000	
Minus: Depreciation	− $18,180	
Adjusted basis:	$171,820	
Plus: Selling expenses	+ $4,000 =	$175,820
Gain on Sale	**$24,180**	

With depreciation recapture along with property appreciation, tax gains can be significant after only several years. One way you can defer these capital gains is by performing a tax exchange. This is the topic of the following section.

1031 Tax Exchanges

The IRS states that "if you exchange a business or investment property solely for business or investment property of a 'like-kind,' no gain or loss is recognized under Internal Revenue Code Section 1031." A successful 1031 exchange thus allows an investor to reinvest all of his or her equity from the sale of a property into the purchase of an allowable replacement property without paying taxes on the gain (including depreciation recapture). The following rules summarize the attributes of a successful 1031 tax exchange:

- Single or multiple properties may be exchanged in the transaction.

- Properties being exchanged must be of "like-kind." "Like-kind" is simply defined as "for investment purposes." Personal residences are thus excluded.

- The property you are receiving must be of the same or greater value than the property you are relinquishing.

- You must identify your replacement property within a 45-day period from the time of the sale of the property you are trading in.

- You must close the transaction on your replacement property within a 180-day period from the sale of the property you are trading in.

One of the more interesting conditions is that the 1031 rule permits you to receive property that has not yet been built. There are several ways that new construction is handled in an exchange.

- You can contract with a builder to purchase the property, which will be completed and ready to close prior to the end of the 180-day exchange period.

- You can purchase the land prior to construction as one of your replacement properties (land is a "like-kind" investment and thus qualifies).

- You can purchase the land and building from the builder at the time of closing.

Tax exchanges thus offer extraordinary advantages, especially after you have accumulated a great amount of equity and depreciation that cannot otherwise be realized without paying taxes on capital gains and depreciation recapture. For example you can "trade up" and exchange several properties for a bigger apartment complex. You can exchange your properties if you are moving to a different geographic area. You can trade your properties for a piece of land and build a new investment property on that land. In short, there are not many other ways to escape capital gains and depreciation recapture when it comes to selling an investment property.

Summary

- Using a flat fee MLS service is a good way to obtain MLS exposure and save on realtor commissions.

- Selling FSBO is not recommended unless you can have property exposure on the MLS.

- Depreciation recapture can greatly add to your taxable gain, especially if you owned your property for many years.

- One way you can defer these capital gains is by performing a tax exchange.

BOOKKEEPING AND COMPUTERS

Real estate investing in the twenty-first century requires you to become skilled at using a computer. Computers are more accurate and they save you time. The world around you will continue to use computers and advance them. Written checks will eventually become a thing of the past. Hand-written tax returns probably won't even exist in the near future. Computers are also a fantastic and indispensable tool for analyzing real estate deals, paying taxes, and most importantly, for keeping and organizing your records.

Organizing

For simplicity, I am assuming that you took my earlier advice and elected to have your properties managed professionally. If you manage your properties yourself, you will need to keep track of far more things, such as tenant phone numbers, lease expiry dates, security deposit records, maintenance paper trails, and late rent checks. For the property owners that choose to handle everything themselves, I refer you to one of the many good books out there that are dedicated solely to this topic. For the rest of us, by having our properties managed, our organizational needs are greatly simplified. Whether you use a computer or a manual record system, you will need to organize and retrieve information such as the maintenance expenses for each unit, the taxes and insurance you paid, the interest you paid, your management fees, and your overall income. You also need to be able to locate the occasional appliance warranty. Unless you have a good system, if you accumulate many properties you will quickly become buried in paperwork and confusion. As is often the case, there are many right ways to do things, and the same is true with how you organize your rental properties. I will therefore present just one method of organizing your records. You may think of better ways, but this system should serve as a good starting point.

For each property we own, we dedicate a single three-ring binder that is organized into various subject categories. By property, we mean building. If the property is a quadraplex, for tax purposes, the records for all four units can be combined, thus the need for only one binder per property. Within each category, we then use sheet protectors to hold any loose paperwork. Typical categories would include leases, correspondence, insurance, warrantees, mortgage information, etc. In short, we use a category for anything we think we may need to retrieve on short notice. If you use a property management company, in addition to the property-specific binders, you will need to have a separate binder to store the monthly statements. The property binders typically last many years before they fill up. When they fill up, I simply date them, and then start a new one. Expense receipts can also be kept in the property binders, but lately I store them in shoe boxes. We have found that once the information from the receipt is entered into your record system, you rarely need to retrieve the original, unless in the unfortunate case you are audited. At the end of a tax season, I typically file away all the receipts with that year's tax information. The only receipts I may file with a property binder are receipts I will need for purposes of a warranty, or to locate contact information from larger repair jobs. Since your computer program is used to store all the information, with the exception of leases or insurance policies, the actual paperwork you filed is rarely needed. Come tax time, you need only to run a cash flow report on that year's income and expenses for each property to have all the information necessary to prepare your taxes.

One Bank Account

A word of advice here: do not mix your private investments with your rental property investments. In our early days of investing, we were operating under a negative cash flow for many years. We only realized this after consolidating our rental property activities into a single bank account. By using a dedicated bank account for your rental business, you will quickly be alerted if you start running a negative cash flow. Some investors advocate using one account for each property you own. While this is no doubt more accurate, I view this as excessive, especially if you are using an electronic record-keeping system. Finally, be sure to keep a good buffer in your rental account for unexpected emergencies. A good rule of thumb is to maintain a cash reserve of at least three to four times your gross monthly rent.

Financial Computer Programs

We have been using a financial computer program for over eight years now for both our home and our rental properties. When our credit card bills arrive, I simply go online and download all the transactions into my account. Each purchase item is automatically categorized. I have been encouraging my wife to actually stop writing checks and use the credit card due to this ease of automatic data entry. Our mortgage payments are all paid by direct deposit. I have my financial files set up so that I enter all expenses by their tax category (repairs, maintenance, cleaning, management, etc.). We also list the account numbers and contact information for our loans and insurance policies. If there is a warranty on an appliance, I include the warranty information as part of my initial purchase entry. A file search can quickly locate the contact or warranty information. If I suspect that the stopped toilet repair I just paid my handyman for has happened before, I can quickly pull all the repairs, going back years, and quickly recognize any trends. Unless you have a photographic memory, keeping track of such things without a computer is nearly impossible.

The beauty of using these financial programs is that all entries are linked. You only need to click on repairs, for example, to get the details for all repairs you had on any unit or property. I can run such profit-loss statements for each property and store it with my taxes. We have had the same computer program file for the last eight years and can actually retrieve and analyze data back that far. Shown in Appendix C is an actual copy of a computer-generated financial report for a cash flow on a typical duplex rental property.

Whether or not you use an accountant, a tax program, or both, having all the data organized in an electronic format will greatly simplify your management duties. It will also be invaluable for retrieving information quickly without having to maintain and sort through a lot of paperwork.

Summary

- It is important to have a separate bank account for your rental properties so you can monitor profit and loss.

- Using a financial accounting program will greatly simplify things come tax time, as it stores all the information you need to fill out your Schedule E.

- Financial accounting programs are also invaluable for quickly retrieving information such as warranties, repair records, and loan information without having to store paperwork.

GLOSSARY

A

active participation. Active participation applies to taxpayers who are not real estate professionals. Active participation is a less stringent standard than material participation. If you own at least a 10% interest in a rental property and are making management decisions, you will qualify as an active participant investor. There is no special test or hourly requirement to fulfill to be an active participant. Active participants can deduct up to $25,000 in losses against non-passive (ordinary) income, subject to the $150,000 MAGI limitation.

adjustable rate mortgage (ARM). An adjustable rate mortgage is where the interest rate on the note is periodically adjusted based on an index. Consequently, payments made by the borrower change over time with the changing interest rate.

adjusted basis. To determine the adjusted basis, take the basis (cost of the property), add the cost of any capital improvements made to the property during the taxpayer's ownership, and subtract any depreciation taken on the property during the same time period. Once the adjusted basis is known, gain or loss can be determined on a sale or exchange of a property.

affordable housing.   A rental unit where the rent is affordable to those living in that housing unit. In the United States and Canada, a commonly accepted guideline for housing affordability is a housing cost that does not exceed 30% of a household's gross income. Income is defined as "low-income," meaning the household earns below 80% of the area median income (AMI).

amortization.   The distribution of a single lump sum into many smaller cash flow installments, as determined by an amortization schedule. Unlike other repayment models, each repayment install-ment consists of both principal and interest. A greater amount of the payment is applied to interest at the beginning of the amortiza-tion schedule, while more money is applied to principal at the end.

amortization schedule.   An amortization schedule is a table detailing each periodic payment on a mortgage and showing the principal and interest portion of each payment. An amortization schedule reveals the specific dollar amount put toward interest and principal balance with each payment.

B

basis.   Your basis is generally the original cost of your property. For tax purposes, the adjusted basis is used to determine gain or loss on the sale or exchange of the property.

balloon payment.   A balloon payment refers to a mortgage that does not fully amortize over the term of the note, thus leaving a balance due before the loan is paid off. The final payment is called a balloon payment because of its large size. Balloon payment mortgages are more common in commercial real estate than in residential real estate. An example of a balloon payment mortgage is the seven-year Fannie Mae Balloon, which features monthly payments based on a thirty-year amortization. When a balloon payment becomes due, either the loan must be paid in full or the borrower needs to refinance the loan.

buyer's agent. A buyer's agent, or buyer agency as it is also known, is the practice of real estate brokers (and their agents) representing a buyer in a real estate transaction. In most states, until the 1990s, buyers who worked with an agent of a real estate broker in finding a house were customers of the brokerage, since the broker represented only sellers. Today, if the buyer is working with a broker other than the brokerage that "lists" the property, he or she may choose to enter into a buyer-brokerage agreement to be represented. In some cases, where the law permits dual agency, even the listing broker may represent the buyer.

C

capital expense. *See* **improvement**

capital improvement. *See* **improvement**

capitalization rate (cap rate). A cap rate is a measure of the ratio between the net operating income (NOI) produced and the original price paid to own the asset.

cash flow. Cash flow is the money left over after collecting all your rents and paying off all expenses.

Certified Commercial Investment Member (CCIM). A Certified Commercial Investment Member (CCIM) is a recognized expert in the field of commercial and investment real estate. Of the estimated 125,000 commercial real estate professionals nationwide, only 6% hold the CCIM designation. To earn the CCIM designation, a candidate must first complete four challenging core courses and three elective credits. The candidate must also submit a portfolio of qualifying transactions. The candidate then must successfully pass a day-long comprehensive examination that is administered twice annually, in the spring and in the fall.

commercial loan.   A short- or long-term renewable loan used to finance a business or rental property. Commercial loans may be amortized but typically have a balloon payment due after a period of time. Commercial loans are typically required for any building with more than four units.

comparative sale.   The comparative sales approach is one of three different appraisal methods used to value real estate. The comparative sales approach attempts to compare a subject property's value with similar (comparable) properties and adjust the value of the subject property according to the presence or absence of value-determining attributes.

conforming loan.   The short definition is that a conforming loan is a loan that meets bank funding criteria. Because of its stake in the mortgage market and because of its history, Fannie Mae and Freddie Mac determine the rules that need to be met for a loan to conform. This is because both Fannie Mae and Freddie Mac will only buy loans that are conforming, to repackage into the secondary market, making the demand for a non-conforming loan much less.

conventional loan.   A mortgage in which the interest rate does not change during the entire term of the loan, also called a Fixed-Rate Mortgage (FRM). Conventional loans can be made to purchase or refinance homes with first and second mortgages on single-family to four-family homes.

D

debt coverage ratio (DCR). A debt coverage ratio (DCR), also known as the debt service coverage ratio, is used to gauge an income property's ability to cover its monthly mortgage payments. If a property has a debt coverage ratio of less than one, the income that property generates is not enough to cover the mortgage payments and the property's operating expenses. However, if a property has a debt coverage ratio of more than one, the property does generate enough revenue to cover annual debt payments.

deed. A deed is a legal instrument used to grant a right. The deed is best known as the method of transferring title to real estate from one person to another, often using a description of its "metes and bounds."

deed of trust. *See* **mortgage.**

demographics. Demographics is a shorthand term for "population characteristics." Demographics include race, age, income, mobility, educational attainment, home ownership, employment status, and location. Demographics are primarily used in economic and marketing research.

depreciation. Depreciation is a deduction the IRS allows you to take on the improvements of your real estate investment. Residential rental property can be depreciated over 27.5 years (assuming a straight-line depreciation method). Only the portion of a property's value that is attributable to the building(s) and not the land can be depreciated.

depreciation recapture. When a rental property is sold at a gain, the IRS requires you to "pay back" all depreciation deductions you took, or could have taken, in prior years. This is done by subtracting the total amount that you depreciated over the years from your basis.

duel agency. Dual agency occurs when the same brokerage represents both the seller and the buyer under written agreements.

E

earnest money. The deposit money given to the seller or his agent by the buyer upon the signing of the agreement of sale to show that he is serious about buying the house. If the sale is transacted, the earnest money is applied against the down payment. If the sale falls through due to the buyer not fulfilling the contractual obligations, the earnest money may be forfeited or lost.

F

Federal Home Loan Mortgage Corporation (Freddie Mac). The Federal Home Loan Mortgage Corporation (Freddie Mac) is a publicly traded company chartered by the U.S. federal government to purchase mortgages and related securities, and then to issue securities and bonds in financial markets backed by those mortgages in secondary markets. Freddie Mac, like its competitor Fannie Mae, is regulated by the Office of Federal Housing Enterprise Oversight (OFHEO) in the U.S. Department of Housing and Urban Development.

Federal National Mortgage Association (Fannie Mae). A publicly traded company chartered by the United States, Fannie Mae is readily available to purchase mortgages, and then issue securities and bonds in financial markets backed by those mortgages in the secondary markets. Because of its stake in the mortgage market, and because of its history, Fannie Mae and its competitor Freddie Mac determine the rules that need to be met for a loan to be a conforming loan. Fannie Mae, is regulated by the Office of Federal Housing Enterprise Oversight (OFHEO) in the U.S. Department of Housing and Urban Development (HUD).

fix-rate mortgage (FRM). *See* **conventional loan**

G

general warranty deed.   A deed that conveys not only all the grantor's interests in—and title to—the property to the grantee, but also warrants that if the title is defective or has a "cloud" on it (such as mortgage claims, tax liens, title claims, judgments, or mechanic's liens against it), the grantee may hold the grantor liable.

G.I. bill.   The G.I. Bill of Rights Act of 1944 provided for college or vocational education for returning World War II veterans (commonly referred to as General Infantry, or G.I.s), as well as one year of unemployment compensation. It also provided loans for returning veterans to buy homes and start businesses.

gross rent multiplier.   The gross rent multiplier is the ratio of the price of a rental property to its annual or monthly gross rents. Gross rent multipliers calculated based upon annual gross rents also indicate the number of years a property would take to pay for itself in gross received rent.

I

improvement. An improvement adds to the value of property, prolongs its useful life, or adapts it to new uses. If you make an improvement to property, the cost of the improvement must be capitalized (depreciated) over the life of the improvement. Examples of improvements include additions, new roofs, wiring upgrades, and wall-to-wall carpeting.

interest-only loan. An interest-only loan is a loan in which the borrower pays only the interest on the principal balance, with the principal balance remaining unchanged. Interest-only loans have lower payments because the borrower does not need to make principal payments.

Internal Revenue Code §469 (IRC §469). Prior to 1986, a taxpayer could generally deduct all his or her real estate losses in full from his or her ordinary income. Since some real estate deductions are just "paper losses," like building depreciation, this gave rise to significant numbers of tax shelters that allowed taxpayers to deduct non-economic losses against ordinary wages and investment income. The Tax Reform Act of 1986 added IRC §469, which, among other things, defined real estate as a passive activity and limited the taxpayer's ability to deduct real estate losses. This code established the current rules governing rental activities, such as the $25,000 passive income loss exclusion. In 1994 real estate professionals were exempted from these loss limitations if they met certain tests put forth by the IRS.

L

loan to value (LTV). The loan to value ratio (LTV) is a factor that lenders consider before they approve a mortgage. LTV is the loan amount expressed as a percentage of either the purchase price or the appraised value for the property. Lenders can require borrowers of high LTV loans to pay private mortgage insurance (PMI) to protect the lender from buyer default, which increases the costs of the mortgage.

M

market cap rates. A market cap rate is determined by evaluating the financial data of similar properties that have recently sold in a specific market. Once the market cap rate is known, value or price may be determined (see **cap rate**).

market rent. Market rents are not actual rents, but rather estimated rents based upon other comparable units. The actual rents may be lower or higher than the market rents.

market value. In the United States, a definition of market values, or fair market values, can be found on the Fannie Mae residential appraisal forms, such as the FNMA 1025, which states the following: The most probable price which a property should bring in a competitive and open market under all conditions requisite to a fair sale, the buyer and seller, each acting prudently, knowledgeably and assuming the price is not affected by undue stimulus. Implicit in this definition is the consummation of a sale as of a specified date and the passing of title from seller to buyer under conditions whereby: (1) buyer and seller are typically motivated; (2) both parties are well informed or well advised, and each acting in what he or she considers his or her own best interest; (3) a reasonable time is allowed for exposure in the open market; (4) payment is made in terms of cash in U. S. dollars or in terms of financial arrangements comparable thereto; and (5) the price represents the normal consideration for the property sold unaffected by special or creative financing or sales concessions granted by anyone associated with the sale.

material participation.   IRC §469 provides that if the taxpayer works on a regular and continual basis in a business, losses are non-passive, i.e., losses are deductible in full against ordinary (non–real estate) income. If a taxpayer does not materially participate, losses are passive and are only deductible up to your passive income limit, and not deductible against ordinary income.

modified adjusted gross income (MAGI).   The MAGI is simply your AGI computed without any passive losses and several other modifiers.

mortgage.   A mortgage is a method of using property (real or personal) as security for the payment of a debt.

mortgage constant.   An amortized loan has in each payment an interest and a principal component. For example, if you borrow a $100,000 at 6% amortized over 30 years, your monthly payment (PI) will be $600. The annual payment would be $600 x 12= $7,200. The ratio of your annual payment to the loan amount is the mortgage constant.

multiple listing service (MLS).   A database that allows real estate brokers representing sellers under a listing contract to widely share information about properties with real estate brokers who may represent potential buyers or wish to cooperate with a seller's broker in finding a buyer for the property. The MLS combines the listings of all available properties that are represented by brokers who are both members of that MLS system and of NAR or CREA (the National Association of Realtors in the United States or the Canadian Real Estate Association).

N

national association of realtors (NAR). The NAR, whose members are known as realtors, is North America's largest trade association, representing over one million members (as reported in 2006). NAR's membership is composed of residential and commercial real estate brokers, real estate salespeople, property managers, appraisers, counselors, and others engaged in all aspects of the real estate industry, where a state license to practice is required.

net operating income (NOI). Net operating income (NOI) is your total income minus your total expenses, where total income is gross rents minus predicted vacancy rate.

non-conforming loan. A non-conforming loan is a term sometimes referred to for loans that do not conform to the Freddie Mac or Fannie Mae guidelines. An example of non-conforming loans would be "jumbo" loans or loans on commercial real estate.

non-passive income. Income from a business in which the taxpayer materially participates is considered non-passive. The following are generally considered sources of non-passive income: ordinary income from salaries, wages, portfolio income, stock gains, sale of undeveloped land, and royalties.

P

passive activity. Prior to 1986 you could deduct your real estate losses from your ordinary income. As part of the 1986 tax reform act, rental real estate activities were separated out and defined as a passive activity. The result is that now real estate tax losses may only be used to offset real estate gains (they cannot be used to offset your ordinary income).

passive income.   Passive income can only be generated from a passive activity. There are only two sources of passive income: a rental activity or a business in which the taxpayer did not materially participate.

Private Mortgage Insurance (PMI). Private Mortgage Insurance is generally required in the United States for home loans that are greater than 80% of the appraised value of the home (less than 20% down payment). PMI is a credit enhancement that permits borrowers to get into homes sooner and with less money down. Typically, PMI is paid monthly with a mortgage payment.

R

realtor.   A realtor is a real estate salesperson or broker who is a member of the National Association of Realtors (NAR). All realtors are brokers/salespersons, but not all brokers/salespersons are realtors.

real estate.   A legal term that encompasses land along with anything permanently affixed to the land, such as buildings. Real estate (immovable property) is often considered synonymous with real property (also sometimes called realty), in contrast with personal property (movable property).

real estate agent.   A real estate agent is a professional who has obtained either a real estate salesperson's license or a real estate broker's license.

real estate broker. After gaining some years of experience in real estate sales, a real estate salesperson may decide to become licensed as a real estate broker. Upon obtaining a broker's license, a real estate agent may continue to work for another broker in a similar capacity as before (often referred to as a broker associate or associate broker) or take charge of his or her own brokerage and hire other salespersons (or broker) licensees.

real estate bubble. A type of economic bubble that occurs periodically in local or global real estate markets.

real estate salesperson. When a person first becomes licensed to become a real estate agent, he or she obtains a real estate salesperson's license from the state in which he or she will practice. To obtain a real estate license, the candidate must take specific coursework (between forty and ninety hours) and then pass a state exam on real estate law and practice. In order to work, salespersons must then be associated with (and act under the authority of) a real estate broker.

repairs. A repair keeps your property in good operating condition. It does not materially add to the value of your property or substantially prolong its life. Repainting your property inside or out, fixing gutters or floors, fixing leaks, plastering, and replacing broken windows are examples of repairs.

replacement cost approach. The replacement cost approach is one of the three commonly used methods to predict the value of real estate. Sometimes referred to as the reproduction method, it is the land value, plus the cost to reconstruct any improvements, less the depreciation on those improvements. This approach is typically most reliable when used on newer structures, but the method tends to become less reliable as properties grow older.

reproduction method. *See* replacement cost approach

return on investment (ROI). Return on investment is a broad term that encompasses all means in which real estate produces wealth, for example, cash flow, appreciation, loan reduction due to amortization, and tax savings.

S

Section 8 Housing. Section 8 is a type of federal assistance provided by the U.S. federal government dedicated to sponsoring subsidized housing for low-income families and individuals. It is formally known as the Housing Choice Voucher Program, but is still commonly referred to as simply Section 8.

seller's agent. In the United States, real estate brokers and their salespersons (commonly called real estate agents) assist sellers in marketing their property and selling it for the highest possible price under the best terms. Seller's agents represent only the seller's interests.

stated cap rate. The stated cap rate sometimes refers to a cap rate on a property that has been estimated by the seller or seller's agent. Such cap rates are often inflated, as they may not accurately represent the true income and expenses of a property. These inflated stated cap rates will artificially inflate the value of an investment property.

T

tax exchange (1031 tax exchange). A 1031 tax exchange, also known as a "like-kind" exchange, is a transaction under U.S. law that specifies that if an asset (usually some form of real estate such as land or a building) is sold and the proceeds of the sale are then reinvested in a like-kind asset, then no gain or loss is recognized, allowing the deferment of capital gains taxes that would otherwise have been due on the first sale. This law is defined by section 1031 of the Internal Revenue Code.

title. The rights of ownership and possession of particular property. In real estate, title may refer to the instruments or documents by which a right of ownership is established (title documents), or it may refer to the ownership interest one has in the real estate.

title insurance. Protection from lenders or homeowners against loss of their interest in property due to legal defects in title.

title search or examination. A check of the title records, generally at the local courthouse, to make sure the buyer is purchasing a house from the legal owner and there are no liens, overdue special assessments, or other claims or outstanding restrictive covenants filed in the record that would adversely affect the marketability or value of title.

APPENDIX A: TOTAL OPERATING EXPENSES

Estimating operating expenses as 45% of gross rents is based upon our historical experience as well as unofficial data from banks we have worked with. This estimate is also supported by the U.S. Census POMS survey. That study they reported total operating expenses in absolute dollars. These dollar values were then converted to percent values using the gross rents reported in the same survey. The median asking rents at the time of the POMS survey were $400–$500 for small- and medium-sized apartments (1–49 units) and $500-$600 per month for large apartments (>50 units). Using this conversion, we obtain a total operating expense of 38%–48% for all units, 38%–48% for small apartment buildings, 43%–54% for medium apartment buildings, and 46%–55% for large apartment complexes.

Yearly Total Operating Expenses by Unit

Total Operating

Costs Per Unit	Total	1–4 Units	5–49 Units	>50 Units
Costs per unit*	$2,300	$2,300	$2,600	$3,300
Costs as a percent of rental income	38%–48%	38%–48%	43%–54%	46%–55%
Mid-range	43%	43%	48.5%	50.5%

Source: "Property Owners and Managers Survey (POMS)" by US Census 2000.

Using percent averages based on gross rents should be used only as an approximation. Actual percent ratios would be expected to vary depending on building type and age and the number of units per building, as well as the location effect on rents.

APPENDIX B:
MAINTENANCE, REPAIRS,
AND RESERVES

In order to more precisely estimate the total operating expenses of a rental property, we must determine the costs of the variable expenses such as repairs, maintenance, and annual reserves. The full equation for total operating expenses looks like:

$$\text{Operating Expenses} = \frac{\text{Taxes} + \text{Insurance} + \text{Yearly Reserves}}{+ \text{Maintenance} / \text{Repairs} + \text{Utilities} + \text{Other}}$$

Fixed expenses, such as taxes, insurance, and utilities, are easy to obtain, but where does one obtain the numbers for "Yearly Reserves" or "Maintenance/Repair costs"? The POMS report estimated that for the average landlord, 14–18% of gross rents went toward maintenance and repairs. If you don't have any data on this figure, this is a good estimate to plug into the equation above. Over the years, we have compiled tables that are highly useful for estimating these variable expenses when estimating cash flows on a potential investment. The following section has tables of proposed expenses to substitute for yearly reserves, maintenance, and repair costs on one to four units.

The first of these tables is presented below. Shown in Table 1 are the monthly expenses required to replace appliances, roofs, carpets, etc.— the so-called yearly reserve requirements.

Table 1: Itemized Yearly Reserves Required

Item	Cost	Frequency (in years)	Yearly Cost
Stove	$350	10 yr	$35
Refrigerator	$400	10 yr	$40
Dishwasher	$350	6 yr	$58
A/C	$1,400	15 yr	$93
Water Heater	$400	7 yr	$57
Furnace	$1,400	15 yr	$93
Carpet (100 yd x $12)	$1,200	7 yr	$171
Roof	$3,500	25 yr	$140
Total			$687/year

If we extrapolate the total cost of $687 per unit to multiple units, we obtain:

Table 2: Total Yearly Reserves Required by Unit

No. Units/Building	Cost/Year
1	$687*
2	$1,234
3	$1,781
4	$2,328

Note that there is only one roof to repair on a multi-unit building, so we can deduct $140 from $687 and add $547 for each additional unit.

These tables can thus be used to estimate your yearly reserves. Next, one needs to estimate the amount of yearly expenses expected from maintenance and repairs.

Table 3: Yearly Maintenance and Repairs Required Activity Per unit

Common area maintenance	$150
Paint	$250
General Repairs	$500
Supplies	$300
Lease-up fees	$200
Total	$1,400/unit

Interestingly, these numbers match up well with the actual numbers received from the POMs report on maintenance, where maintenance expenses were reported as a percentage of gross rents. Assuming a rent of $600[15] per unit, or $7,200 per year, and using a yearly estimate for repairs/maintenance of $1,400 per unit from Table 3, one obtains a value of 19% ($7,200/$1,400). The POMS study reported 14–18%, depending on the number of units (see Appendix E). Another useful presentation is where the yearly reserves *and* maintenance/repair expenses are combined on a per unit basis.

Table 4: Total Maintenance/Repairs and
Yearly Reserves Required by Unit

No. Units/Building	Estimated Cost/Year
1	$2,087
2	$4,034
3	$5,981
4*	$7,928

*For each unit after 4, simply add $1,947 ($547 for yearly
reserves and $1,400 for maintenance and repairs).

Unless your units are very old and are in need of renovation, you
mustn't normally include a renovation expense in your calculations.
However, if your units are in poor shape, you may want to consider
adding the cost of renovations into your expense formula and see if
the property still cash flows. Also, if you plan on keeping your properties for twenty years or more, you may need to eventually deal with
these expenses.

Table 5: Renovation Costs Per Unit

Item	Cost	Frequency	Annualized ($)
Kitchen	$5,000	30 yr	$166
Bath x 2	$6,000	30 yr	$200
Electrical	$3,000	30 yr	$75
Plumbing	$2500	30 yr	$83
Windows	$2,000	30 yr	$66
Doors	$1000	20 yr	$50
Drywall/Paint	$2,000	40 yr	$40
Driveways/ Parking Area	$5,000	40 yr	$125
Siding Replacement	$5,000	40 yr	$125
Total			$930/unit/year

Table 6: Renovation Costs Per Unit (Annualized)

No. Units	Estimated Cost/Year ($)
1	$930
2	$1,610
3	$2,290
4	$2,970
Multiple units:	Add $680/unit*

*It was assumed that parking and siding replacement would be the same for 1–4 units, thus these costs were not included for multi-unit complexes.

As a final comment, this information is provided only as a guide. You are encouraged to adjust for inflation or local building or handyman costs, and generate your own costs tables for your geographic location. The overall approach, however, should prove helpful in calculating more accurate cash flows for your prospective purchases. These numbers are especially useful when used along with one of the many cash flow analysis programs available. Once you obtain accurate values for these variable expenses, you can then just substitute in the correct values when performing cash flow calculations.

APPENDIX C:
TYPICAL COMPUTER-
GENERATED CASH FLOW

Report for Duplex

INCOME		
Income	14,870.00	100.00 %
TOTAL INCOME	14,870.00	100 %
EXPENSES		
Management	957.41	7.03 %
Real Estate Interest	6,674.94	49.00 %
Repair	403.22	2.96 %
Taxes and Insurance	2,193.16	16.10 %
Utilities	213.25	1.57 %
To 1501 Collegeview Mortgage	3,181.06	23.35 %
TOTAL EXPENSES	13,623.04	100 %
OVERALL TOTAL	1,246.96	100 %

APPENDIX D: INSPECTION REPORT

Property Address:

Exterior	Needed Repairs	Cost
Landscaping		
Steps/Railings		
Driveway/Walks		
Fence		
Storage Areas		
Sewer/Septic		
Roof		
Decks/Patios		
Foundation/Crawl		
Exterior Siding		
Mailboxes		
Gutters		
Other		

Living Room		
Walls/Ceilings		
Doors/Locks		
Window/Treatment		
Carpet/Flooring		
Electrical Outlets		
Other		

Kitchen

Walls/Ceiling _____ _____

Countertops _____ _____

Doors/Locks _____ _____

Window/Treatment _____ _____

Sink/Under Sink _____ _____

Appliances _____ _____

Furnace/Filter _____ _____

A/C _____ _____

Water Heater _____ _____

Oven _____ _____

Dishwasher _____ _____

Disposal _____ _____

Smoke Detector _____ _____

Garage Door _____ _____

Other _____ _____

Bedroom 1

Walls/Ceiling _____ _____

Doors/Locks _____ _____

Flooring _____ _____

Window/Treatment _____ _____

Other _____ _____

Bathroom 1

Walls/Ceiling _____ _____

Window/Treatment _____ _____

Shower/Tub _____ _____

Doors/Locks _____ _____

Sink/Under Sink _____ _____

Cabinets/Fixtures _____ _____

Fan/Lighting _____ _____

Other _____ _____

Bedroom 2
Walls/Ceiling
Doors/Locks
Flooring
Window/Treatment
Other

Bathroom 2
Walls/Ceiling
Window/Treatment
Shower/Tub
Doors/Locks
Sink/Under Sink
Cabinets/Fixtures
Fan/Lighting
Other

Bedroom 3
Walls/Ceiling
Doors/Locks
Flooring
Window/Treatment
Other

Bathroom 3
Walls/Ceiling
Window/Treatment
Shower/Tub
Sink/Under Sink
Doors/Locks
Cabinets/Fixtures
Fan/Lighting
Other

Bedroom 4

Walls/Ceiling _____ _____

Doors/Locks _____ _____

Flooring _____ _____

Window/Treatment _____ _____

Other _____ _____

Bathroom 4

Walls/Ceiling _____ _____

Window/Treatment _____ _____

Shower/Tub _____ _____

Sink/Under Sink _____ _____

Doors/Locks _____ _____

Cabinets/Fixtures _____ _____

Fan/Lighting _____ _____

Other _____ _____

APPENDIX E:
MAINTENANCE COST AS A
PERCENTAGE OF INCOME

The POMS data was reported as a median percent range of 14–18% of gross rental income. If you plot all the data for all apartment sizes in the survey, you can observe that the actual spread in maintenance expenses is quite huge. For example, in looking at the 2-unit case, you can see that >5% of the total respondents paid "none" on maintenance, 15% paid 1–4%, a little under 20% paid 5–9%, and 5% paid > 75% on maintenance that year. Clearly the conservative investor should plan for the "center of the bell curve" averages, but keep reserves for the unexpected "high maintenance" years.

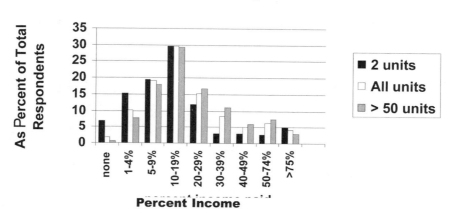

Percent Rental Income Spent on Maintenance by Unit

Source: "Property Owners and Managers Survey (POMS)" by U.S. Census 2000

Notes

[1] According to the National Association of Realtors, for the period of 1963–2005, home-value appreciation outpaced consumer price inflation by about 1.5% per year.

[2] U.S. Census Bureau, "Property Owners and Managers Survey (POMS)." Last Revised: December 17, 2004. The following sections summarize the findings of this report found in 'What We Have Learned about Properties, Owners, and Tenants From the Property Owners and Managers Survey" by Howard Savage.

[3] It is very unlikely that the POMS study was just a "bad year" for rental property profitability. In the same survey, over 65% of the owners stated that their property values actually went up or stayed the same and only 12% of the investors reported that property values went down in that year. Additionally, 1995, the year of the survey, was not associated with any type of real estate downturn.

[4] "Housing Characteristics 2000": Census 2000 Brief, 2001, by Jeanne Woodward and Bonnie Damon.

[5] "Multifamily Rental Housing in the 21st Century," Colton, K. W., and Collignon, K.; January 29, 2001.

[6] The actual projections for "all household growth" vs. "multifamily household growth" are, respectively, as follows: 1995–2000 (1.1%, 0.9%); 2000–2005 (1.1%, 1.1%); 2005–2010 (1.1%, 1.2%).

[7] Colton and Collignon, 51.

[8] Garden apartments refer to complexes where several buildings are located on a large lot, as opposed to a high-rise building with little land available as a common area.

[9] Colton and Collignon, 76.

[10] "When are cap rates too high? Too low? Or just right?" by Tad Philipp and Sally Gordon, Moody's Investment Service, March 11, 2003.

[11] At the time of this study, mid-2003.

[12] To understand this 2% "rule of thumb," one needs to understand mortgage constants. The mortgage constant is the yearly PI divided by the loan amount. Thus, for a standard 30-year loan of $100,000 at 6.00%, your (PI) payment would be $599 per month, or $7,188 per year. The mortgage constant is therefore $7,188 / $100,000, or 7.19%. This is 1% higher than your 6% loan because we have included the prin-

cipal in the ratio. This (principal) gap observed between mortgage constant and mortgage interest rates actually closes as interest rates increase. This makes sense because, after all, the gap is due to the principal portion of the loan, and higher interest rates pay less principal Thus, for example, at a 10% interest rate, the mortgage constant is 10.5%. Because of this "principal effect" on amortized commercial loans, it is common practice to generalize and say that your cap rate should be at least 1–2% higher than your interest rate to have profitability.

[13] This range is based upon historical national averages in the United States over the last thirty years. Local averages may differ.

[14] These estimates are provided for informational purposes only. Actual costs may or may not approximate expenses in your situation.

[15] The U.S. median rents at the time of this writing.

INDEX

A

active participation, 189–190

activity, 56, 66, 68, 188, 190, 196

adjustable rate mortgage (ARM), 41, 63, 98, 107, 108, 114, 119, 167

advertising, 25, 70, 143, 145–149, 151, 169, 195, 197, 206

agent, buyer's, 21–24, 28, 132, 134, 137, 206, 207

agent, listing, 21, 22

agent, real estate , 21, 22, 25, 30, 93, 136, 207

agent, seller's, 21–23, 28, 84, 85, 92, 95, 96, 132, 133, 135

amortization, 5, 84, 115–117, 119

apartment, 7, 8, 12–15, 17, 18, 20, 31, 32, 39–44, 49, 51, 55, 60, 61, 63, 69, 73–77, 80, 87, 91–93, 95, 97, 99, 102, 113, 126, 127, 138, 141, 144–150, 156, 162, 165, 166, 170, 173, 175, 180, 204, 211

appreciation, 3–6, 12, 17, 32–35, 37, 38, 54–56, 58, 60–62, 64–67, 70, 85, 87, 92, 97, 103, 108, 114, 118, 142, 209

asset, 37, 100, 125

attorney, 125, 132, 133, 135, 139, 161, 179, 182

B

balloon payment, 101, 113, 126, 136

bank, 2, 4, 81, 95, 99, 115, 126, 141

bank account, 214, 215

broker, 4, 22, 29, 122, 142

building code, 45, 47–49, 139

business, 13, 28, 29, 53, 55, 56, 121, 129, 132, 139, 140, 142, 156, 160, 162, 166, 172, 175, 180–183, 189, 190, 209, 214

C

capital gain, 9, 10, 17, 35, 73, 122, 124, 204, 207–209, 211 capitalization rate (cap rate), 90, 93–106, 110

cash flow, 2–4, 6, 12, 26, 33, 35–38, 41, 42, 44, 51, 54–57, 60, 61, 67–71, 73–75, 77–89, 98, 100–103, 108, 109, 113, 114, 116–123, 127, 129–131, 142, 153–155, 163, 167, 168, 186, 191, 213–215

cash-out refinancing, 121–123, 125, 128

, 3, 14, 26, 37, 45, 54, 62–65, 67, 68, 93, 96, 139

commission, 21–25, 27, 28, 67, 147, 153, 196, 197, 206–209, 211

comparable sales approach. *See* comparative sales approach.

comparative sales approach, 47, 91, 93, 102, 105, 106, 110

condominium, 31, 37, 38, 41, 51, 97, 202

construction, 15, 45–51, 80, 91, 95, 105, 125, 126, 141, 142, 178, 210

country, 24, 35, 62, 67, 68, 96, 155, 163

court, 107, 154, 156, 157, 185, 194

credit, 19, 34, 123, 125, 141, 155, 156, 158, 174, 184, 185, 214

crime, 26, 30, 54, 58, 62, 63, 67–70, 75

D

debt, 3, 5, 76, 78, 81, 93, 95, 102, 115, 118–120, 158

demographics, 13, 15, 17–20, 26, 30, 34, 35, 53, 55, 67, 97, 107, 147, 155

Department of Housing and Urban Development (HUD), 48, 124

depreciation, 35, 37, 38, 57, 61, 62, 75, 86, 105, 191–196, 198–200, 207–211

disclosure form, 134

driving, 25, 26, 30, 63, 67

drugs, 63, 162

due diligence, 129, 136–138, 144

E

earnest deposit, 134, 135, 137

eviction, 8, 40, 153, 155–158, 162

expenses, 2–4, 39–41, 44, 46, 51, 73–84, 87, 93, 94, 96, 103, 109, 130–132, 142, 143, 150, 154, 162–164, 167, 168, 188, 192–196, 198, 204, 208, 209, 212–214

F

fair market value, 73, 89, 90, 206

financing, 31, 33, 45–47, 49, 78–83, 90, 94, 98–102, 107–110, 113–115, 117–121, 123–127, 132, 133, 135–137, 144

fixer-upper, 124

for sale by owner (FSBO), 21, 24, 207, 211

G

gross rent multiplier (GRM), 57–62, 64, 68, 70, 74, 75, 82, 83, 90, 102–106, 110

H

home, manufactured, 48

home, mobile, 37, 38, 48

home, modular, 48–50

homeowners' insurance, 125, 138, 175

house, boarding. *See* house, rooming.

house, rooming, 31, 40, 41, 173

household, single-adult, 20

household, single-parent, 17, 20

housing, affordable, 15–16, 19, 31, 35, 68, 148

housing, assisted, 16

housing, luxury, 31

housing, student, 31, 38, 40, 42, 44, 63, 64, 70, 85, 122, 148, 149, 151, 169, 170, 172–174

I

improvement, 104, 122–124, 150, 151, 163, 167, 191, 193, 194, 196, 200, 204, 208, 209

improvement, capital, 75, 163, 194, 208, 209

income, 2, 3, 8–10, 14–17, 31, 33–35, 38, 41, 47, 51, 54–58, 62, 68, 69, 73, 74, 76–82, 84, 87, 90–96, 98, 103, 104, 106, 110, 147, 149, 171, 177, 187–192, 195, 196, 198–200, 202, 203, 205, 207, 208, 212, 213

inflation, 2–5, 37, 64, 65, 87, 100, 108, 109

inspection, 129–133, 136–139, 144, 147, 172

insurance, 4, 13, 29, 36, 75, 78, 79, 118, 122, 124, 125, 128, 138, 159, 160, 175–181, 183–186, 195–197, 205, 212–214

interest, 5, 17, 33–36, 46, 60, 61, 66, 69, 77, 78, 81–83, 89, 94, 96–102, 107, 108, 110, 113–121, 123, 126–128, 142, 189, 195–197, 204, 212

Internal Revenue Service (IRS), 105, 187, 188, 190–196, 199, 200, 207, 209

Internet, 21, 22, 24, 26, 58, 69, 93, 107, 133, 147–149, 151, 169, 187, 194

investor, 1–5, 7–9, 11, 13, 15, 19–23, 28–34, 36, 45, 47, 49, 50, 51, 54, 55, 62, 63, 65, 67–69, 73, 74, 86, 87, 95–100, 107–109, 113, 120, 121, 127, 128, 132, 133, 168, 177, 187, 202, 204, 205, 209, 214

L

land, 3, 14, 33, 36–38, 51, 53, 65, 86, 104, 105, 126, 168, 191–193, 200, 209–211

landlord, 7, 11, 13, 14, 29, 35, 36, 39, 40, 43, 63, 65, 79–86, 138, 140, 143, 150, 154–157, 159, 161, 166, 167, 169, 175, 178, 181–184, 186, 189, 194, 195, 202

landscaping, 33, 122, 168, 169, 203, 205

lawyer. *See* attorney.

lease, 39–41, 137, 138, 147, 148, 153, 154, 159–162, 172–174, 205, 212, 213

leverage, 3–5, 12, 115, 117, 120, 124, 135

liability, 166, 175, 178–186

limited liability corporation (LLC), 182, 186

loan, 2, 5, 12, 34–36, 46, 69, 77–79, 81, 82, 87, 95, 96, 99, 101, 102, 113–119, 121–124, 126, 127, 141, 142, 158, 215

loan, commercial, 32, 99, 113, 126–128, 136

loan, conventional , 108, 113, 119, 125–128, 136

loan, major. *See* loan, commercial.

location, 13, 37, 53–55, 57, 59–61, 63–67, 69, 71, 104, 148

M

maintenance, 7, 12, 27, 32, 37, 47, 51, 69, 74–79, 82, 83, 122, 131, 143, 150, 163, 170, 195, 197, 212, 214

management, 7, 8, 12, 40–42, 51, 54, 75, 78, 79, 138, 140, 142, 144, 145, 147, 153–161, 163–166, 169, 174, 181, 182, 189, 197, 212–215

market rent, 59, 73–74, 77, 79, 80, 83–85, 87, 131, 141, 143, 147, 149, 150, 151

mortgage, 4, 6, 17, 29, 31, 33, 35, 36, 51, 60, 61, 66, 75, 76, 78, 86, 96–98, 100, 101, 107, 108, 110, 115, 117–119, 122–124, 127, 128, 136, 142, 196, 197, 203, 213, 214

Multiple Listings Service (MLS), 21, 22, 24, 30, 58, 207, 211

N

National Association of Realtors (NAR), 6, 69, 86, 107, 109, 132, 133, 135, 144, 161, 162

negotiation, 23, 106, 130–132, 136, 162

net operating income (NOI), 77–82, 93–97, 100–102

O

Offer to Purchase Contract, 132, 134, 135, 144

P

pets, 8, 40, 153, 159–163, 173, 174

principal, 5, 77, 78, 114–117, 134

Property Owners and Managers Survey (POMS), 6–9, 11, 12, 73–78, 145–147, 150, 151

property value, 3, 54, 58, 65, 91, 94, 95, 97, 99, 102, 137

property, investment , 4, 22, 28, 30, 33, 49, 50, 53, 54, 78, 92, 93, 98, 113, 125, 126, 128, 138, 176, 183–185, 202, 204, 205, 208, 209, 211

property, multifamily, 8–12, 15, 31–33, 35, 36, 38, 41, 43–45, 47, 50, 51, 53, 54, 56, 61, 62, 86, 102, 138, 169, 202

property, personal, 132, 178, 193, 194, 198

property, rental , 1, 2, 5–10, 21, 25, 26, 30–33, 35, 38, 46, 57, 69, 70, 73, 75, 77, 80, 86, 90–92, 118, 119, 126, 140, 146, 159, 166, 169, 170, 175, 177, 179–182, 187–193, 195–202, 206–208, 212, 214, 215

property, residential, 4, 21, 31, 32, 36, 45, 47, 57, 66, 91, 95, 105, 126, 135, 191

property, single-family, 3, 14, 31–36, 38–41, 43–45, 47, 50, 51, 55, 56, 64, 68, 73, 75, 86, 91–93, 101, 102, 106, 110, 113, 127, 136, 169–171, 202, 204

R

real estate bubble, 68, 105, 107–109, 111

realtor, 21–26, 28, 30, 45, 93, 107, 130, 133–135, 139, 141, 147, 161, 206, 211

references, 26, 45, 155, 156, 158, 166

renovation, 27, 46, 74, 82, 136, 141, 142, 168, 187

repair, 33, 36, 39, 47, 51, 69, 74–80, 83, 124, 129–133, 138, 139, 141, 143, 144, 154, 156, 157, 163, 164, 166–168, 170–172, 178, 183, 187, 193–197, 199, 200, 204, 213–215

replacement cost approach, 90, 104–106, 110

reproduction method. *See* replacement cost approach.

retirement, 9–12

S

Schedule E tax form, 196, 197, 215

security deposit, 138, 153, 154, 173, 212

signs, 25, 63, 84, 85, 145, 146, 148, 149, 151

Social Security, 3, 11

stock, 68, 85, 94, 100, 106, 115, 119, 120, 189

stock market, 1, 2, 29, 85, 96, 97, 107, 117

suburbs, 14, 61, 62, 65, 86

T

tax, 5, 6, 12, 14, 17, 19, 26, 30, 35, 36, 45, 75, 78, 79, 84, 87, 93, 105, 106, 118, 122, 125, 163, 182, 187, 189–193, 195, 196–202, 204, 207–215

tax record, 26, 30, 45, 78, 84, 93, 106, 192, 193, 209

tenant, high-risk, 34

tenant, lifestyle, 16, 19

tenant, middle-market, 16, 17

tenant, short-term, 34, 150

total annual debt (TAD), 77–82

townhome, 31, 37, 38, 41, 51, 85, 202

turnover, 36, 39–41, 146, 151, 165, 171, 172

U

utilities, 43, 46, 63, 78, 79, 84, 143, 147, 195, 203

V

vacancy, 26, 30, 33, 36, 40, 42, 43, 45, 47, 56, 59, 63, 64, 74, 78, 79, 81, 83–86, 94, 96, 103–105, 125, 131, 140, 143, 146, 147, 150, 156, 158, 172, 173, 204–206

Z

zoning, 38, 44–48, 50, 67